CULTURE

A Parable for

DRIVES

Living and Leading

SUCCESS

with Purpose

BABAK DEHNAD

Edited by Lil Barcaski

Published by: GWN Publishing
www.GWNPublishing.com

Cover Design: Kristina Conatser

ISBN: 978-1-965971-18-5

DEDICATED TO

the love of my life, Kristal, my daughters Ava and Mila and my furry friends, Molly and Meatball.

TABLE OF CONTENTS

WORDS OF PRAISE FOR "CULTURE DRIVES SUCCESS"

"This book is a must-read for anyone serious about building teams that scale — not just with skills, but with the right culture. As a Talent Acquisition Leader, I know firsthand that hiring for values and alignment is what drives long-term success. This isn't just a book — it's a guide for getting culture right from the start."

— Michelle Ashby, *Talent Acquisition Leader & Executive Search Partner at Forte Search Partners*

"This was the perfect time for me to read Babak's book, so much resonated for me as I am living through similar experiences in my current role as CHRO and Culture Leader. This was life changing. What I like most are the many practical exercises that I tried for myself and experienced immediate positive change personally and professionally. It is helping me closer align my personal and work values in a meaningful way. This is a great tool for all CPO/CHROs to have!"

— Betsy Campbell Barth, *Chief People Officer at FLYR Labs*

"I think of this book being a working manual for a start-up Founder or C-level leaders, it should be required reading."

— Dave Arnold, *President at Arnold Partners*

"Culture Drives Success offers a thoughtful conversation that makes me reflect on how I live, lead, and connect with others. It's a powerful reminder that great leadership starts with intentional culture."

— Zachary Zapata, *Vice President, Engineering at Stockpile*

"Babak was a true partner in shaping the culture at InMobi during a time of global growth and transformation. In this book, he distills that same wisdom into a clear and purposeful guide. It's a must-read for any leader who believes, as I do, that culture is the ultimate competitive advantage."

— Naveen Tewari, *Founder & CEO at InMobi*

"Babak helped us evolve from a product team that moved fast to one that moved smart, together. His impact on our culture was deep and lasting—and this book distills that expertise in a way that's inspiring, practical, and impossible to ignore. Every leader will benefit from it."

— Steve Wilson, *Chief AI and Product Officer at Exabeam*

"Culture is the foundation of wellness, trust, and performance. Babak shows leaders how to build organizations where people thrive—and business follows."

— Darren Brown, *President at New Front*

"Having worked closely with Babak during our high-growth journey at Contrast, I saw firsthand how his approach to culture elevated both people and performance. This book captures that same clarity and intentionality—it's a powerful tool for any leader looking to build with purpose."

— Surag Patel, *Founder & CEO at Pixee*

"The most scalable systems in tech are built on strong engineering—and the most scalable teams are built on strong culture. Culture Drives Success offers a clear and actionable guide for leaders who want to grow with intention, purpose, and people at the center."

— Asim Husain, *Vice President & General Manager at Google Core Developer*

WHY I WROTE THIS BOOK

I have spent an unreasonable amount of time scouring the internet and bookstores for books on culture and self-development. What I found was a staggering number of books written by three types of people: consultants (monetizers), one-percenters (CEOs), and academics (theorists). Consultants write books to market themselves because, let's be honest, it's easier to sell a $25 book than a $25,000 workshop (but that book is just the funnel to sell the workshop and build artificial credibility). Academics write because their job requires them to publish, even if their findings never escape the university bubble. And CEOs? After working with dozens, I've learned they often see the world through a different lens—one shaped by solitude and high stakes. It's why so many call the job lonely. Writing a book might not always resonate with the rest of us, but the best leaders I've seen don't write to impress—they write to express. To distill wisdom, share lessons, and make the journey a little less lonely for the next one in line.

I wanted to write a book that actually helps people, not one that sounds good in a TED Talk but falls apart in real life.

Ever finish a book that promised to change your life in five easy steps, four secrets, or a magic formula? You highlight passages, nod along, maybe even tell a friend, and then what? Nothing happens. Your motivation fizzles, and life goes back to normal. I know this because I've read (or listened to) over 1,000 books on self-help, self-development, self-employment, self-fulfillment, self … fill in the blank. They're inspirational, sure. Therapeutic even. But did they change me? Nope. What was missing that didn't motivate me to take action afterwards? That's the missing piece that set me on the path to write something different, something action-centric.

I tell my daughters, *"You don't learn how to play tennis by reading a book. You get on the court. You don't learn to drive by watching YouTube videos. You get behind the wheel."* And yet, so many self-help books act like just knowing something is the same as doing something. It's not. Change happens when you have the right tools and take action.

The only real change I saw in my own life happened when I approached learning like a student, having a growth mindset—not just absorbing information, but actually using practical tools. Someone wise (Benjamin Franklin) once said: *"Tell me, I forget, show or teach me I may remember, involve me, and I learn."* So where did I find these tools?

For 30 years, I worked in Human Resources in Silicon Valley, which is just a fancy way of saying I was a social scientist in an open-air laboratory. How many people get to run real-life experiments on leadership, culture, and human behavior with actual people? I did. And let me tell you, some of those experiments were spectacular failures. But through trial, error, and *a lot* of tough lessons, I found real, practical tools that actually work. That's why I wrote this book: to give you those tools—without the fluff, without the TED Talk bravado, and without the $5,000 seminar upsell at the end (I do offer a free online tool/assessment).

It's human nature that shapes us and our principles. You don't magically change when you step into a different role. You don't have one set of values at work and another at home. You are who you are, everywhere you go. Yet, so many people choose friendships, relationships, and jobs that go against their core values. They stay in environments that drain them, convince themselves they're happy, and call it "success." But that's not happiness—it's performance. It's the emotional equivalent of auto-tuning your life to make it sound good, even when deep down, you hate the song. The end result is an empty shell of a body and a burnt-out soul by age 50.

This book is for anyone who feels stuck in artificial happiness and wants a way out of that life and a way into a fulfilling one.

And speaking of artificial, I don't mean AI—though, let's be real, AI is about to disrupt our lives in ways we can't even predict. No, I mean the artificial world we've built online—the "more generation." Buy more, make more, do more, Insta more, Snap more, Tik more, Tok more. Social media was meant to connect us, but instead, it's become a highly produced and staged fantasy land where we can pretend to be one-percenters. The truth? Most people aren't okay, but we fake it for the algorithm. The stories we consume are not real. But the expectations they create? Oh, those are *very* real.

I wanted this book to be a reality check, not another set of impossible ideals.

Funny enough, I already wrote a book before this one—a serious, business-oriented book on company culture and leadership. That book is a prescription for business leaders who desperately need guidance, but it's very relevant to all humans as well. It's technically sound but I hate to say it, it's just not as entertaining or fun like this one. Let's face it, we spend most of our waking hours at work, and it's easy to get consumed by it. I did. But when I asked myself who I actually wanted to reach, I realized: not just business leaders.

I wanted to write for humans.

And what do humans remember? Stories. That's why this book is different. Instead of telling you what to do, I'm going to show you through a parable to bring these concepts to life. Because if we can see them play out in someone else's life, we can recognize them on our own.

So, here's my promise to you: This book won't just inspire you—it will equip you. No guru jargon. No empty motivation. Just real, practical tools to help you build a better culture—personally and professionally.

Let's get to work.

HOW TO USE THIS BOOK EFFECTIVELY (WITHOUT FALLING ASLEEP)

THIS IS NOT YOUR TYPICAL SELF-HELP BOOK (MORE LIKE A SELF-DEVELOPMENT BOOK)

If you've ever bought a book promising *5 Steps to Unstoppable Happiness* or *The Secret Formula for Success*, only to finish it and … do absolutely nothing, I feel you.

This is not one of those books.

This is a step-by-step recipe for fulfillment but think of it less like a rigid baking recipe (where one wrong measurement ruins the whole thing) and more like making a legendary stew—one that takes time, the right ingredients, and your own personal flair.

Why? Because happiness is like instant coffee. Fulfillment is like a slow-brewed espresso.

We're going to restructure your life—at home, at work, and in your mind—so that fulfillment isn't something you chase but something you live.

And unlike those books that make you feel guilty for not having a perfect morning routine (because let's be honest, some days you just want to roll out of bed and survive on caffeine fumes), I'm going to give you **real,**

practical, science-backed, human-tested strategies that don't require you to become a Zen monk or quit your job to "find yourself."

THE THREE SECTIONS OF THIS BOOK (A ROADMAP TO A LIFE THAT DOESN'T SUCK)

This book is divided into three sections, each designed to take you on a journey from personal transformation to professional excellence—and finally, to an arsenal of tools you can use to keep growing.

Section 1: YOU – Personal Culture & Building a Life That Works

Before we fix the big, scary external world, we start with the one thing **you** can control—yourself.

This section is about **designing your personal culture**. You have one, so let's look at what defines yours. Are you the type of person who wakes up at 5 AM, meditates, and makes homemade almond butter?

Or are you the person who hits snooze eight times and wonders why life feels chaotic?

Either way, your daily rituals, mindset, and choices create your personal culture.

Here, you'll learn to:

- Identify what actually fulfills you (spoiler: it's not just money or status).
- Unlearn toxic habits that keep you stuck in survival mode.
- Design rituals that create meaning, not just productivity.
- Build a mindset that fosters growth, resilience, and purpose.
- Create a life that feels aligned instead of one that just looks good on Instagram.

Think of this section as spring cleaning for your soul.

Section 2: WORK — Professional Culture & Creating a Career That Matters

Once you've built a personal foundation, it's time to tackle your work/professional culture.

Like it or not, you spend more time working than doing anything else. (Yes, even more than binge-watching Netflix.)

So, if you hate your work culture, you're going to be miserable.

This section is about understanding and shaping your professional culture so that:

- You fit in AND belong (because those are two different things).
- You share a common purpose with your company, rather than just trading hours for a paycheck.
- You develop leadership skills that create an environment where people actually want to work.
- You learn how to navigate workplace dysfunction (without quitting and moving to a remote cabin in the woods).

Work is not just about what you do—it's about how you do it and *who* you do it with.

This section will show you how to create a culture of fulfillment in your professional life, whether you're leading a company, managing a team, or just trying to survive corporate nonsense.

Section 3: TOOLS — The Ultimate Culture Toolkit (Plus a Free Culture Assessment!)

You've worked on yourself. You've reshaped your professional life.

Now, you need the tools to keep it all together.

This section is your go-to reference manual—filled with templates, exercises, checklists, frameworks and frequently asked questions to help you maintain and build on what you've learned.

- A FREE online culture assessment to diagnose and improve your work culture.

- Workplace tools—sample strategies, team-building exercises, and hiring frameworks to create a people-first culture.

- Self-improvement hacks to reinforce the habits you developed in Section 1.

- A roadmap to sustaining fulfillment—because we all have setbacks, and you'll want to get back on track when life inevitably throws you off.

This section is like your personal Swiss Army knife for culture-building—whether at home, at work, or anywhere in between.

THE RULES OF ENGAGEMENT (HOW TO ACTUALLY USE THIS BOOK)

This book is designed to be used, not just read. Here's how:

1. Stories That Stick

Ava's journey isn't just entertainment—it's your mental shortcut to remembering these lessons when you need them.

Think of it like this: You'll remember Abdi's desert story about values way more than you'd remember a corporate PowerPoint on "Core Leadership Principles."

2. Practical Exercises (The "Get Off Your Butt" Section)

Each chapter has exercises designed to push you out of your comfort zone and make the lessons *stick*.

> **EXAMPLE:** *You won't just read about values—you'll test them in real life.*

3. Unconventional Exercises (For Those Who Like a Challenge)

These aren't your typical self-improvement tasks.

- Some will be **uncomfortable.**
- Some will be **funny.**
- Some will make **you rethink everything.**

> **EXAMPLE:** *One challenge might require you to speak only when necessary for an entire day. (Spoiler alert: You'll realize how much unnecessary noise you create.)*

4. Five Practical Tools Per Chapter (No Fluff, Just Gold)

Every chapter ends with five things you can apply immediately—at home and at work.

Why? Because remembering 20+ steps is ridiculous, but remembering five? Easy.

5. Neuroscience Facts (Because Science is Cool)

I'll break down the actual biology behind why these principles work.

Your mindset shapes your culture. The way you think determines the way you act, which influences the way people interact with you. Leaders with a growth mindset create cultures of innovation; leaders with a fixed mindset create cultures of fear.

Your brain loves patterns. Culture is reinforced through repetition—rituals, habits, behaviors. The more you practice certain values, the more they become who you are. Just like muscles strengthen with use, cultural habits become automatic over time.

Gratitude rewires your brain. Studies show that daily gratitude rituals can literally rewire neural pathways to make you happier, more optimistic, and even physically healthier. Organizations that celebrate small wins and recognize people regularly create cultures of motivation and resilience.

Your environment affects your mindset. Just like cluttered spaces can overwhelm the brain, a toxic work environment can rewire your nervous system to stay in stress mode. Leaders who create psychological safety allow people to focus on growth instead of survival.

Trust reduces stress and increases performance. High-trust cultures produce more oxytocin, the bonding chemical that fosters connection and loyalty. Low-trust cultures flood employees with cortisol, the stress hormone that fuels burnout.

6. Conclusion & Takeaways (For Your Cheat Sheet Moments)

At the end of each chapter, I'll wrap it up with key insights to remind you what matters.

> **EXAMPLE:** *If you only take one thing from Chapter 1, it should be: "Your values are your compass. Ignore them, and you'll always feel lost."*

CULTURE IS A MINDSET—IT'S PART OF OUR NATURE

Culture isn't just what we do—it's how we think. It's the mindset we bring to every situation, every challenge, every interaction.

The strongest cultures—whether in families, companies, or communities—aren't built on random behaviors. They're built on deliberate mindsets.

MINDSET IS THE FOUNDATION OF CULTURE

If you want to change a culture, you have to change how people think first.

Want a culture of excellence? Develop a mindset of continuous learning.

Want a culture of resilience? Train your mind to see failures as lessons, not roadblocks.

Want a culture of belonging? Foster a mindset of inclusion and empathy.

Culture isn't just what we do—it's how we see the world.

And that starts in the mind.

THE BIOLOGY OF HAPPINESS: WHY YOUR BRAIN IS A DRUG DEALER

Before we talk about fulfillment, we need to understand happiness—because your brain is basically running a four-drug operation.

1. Dopamine: The Quick Fix (a.k.a. The Amazon Prime Effect)

Dopamine is the achievement chemical—the rush you get when you:

- Open a package (even if you forgot what you ordered)
- Check off a to-do list item
- Hit a work milestone
- Get a "like" on social media

It's short-lived, but addictive. If you're stuck in the loop of chasing more, more, more, congratulations—you're a dopamine junkie.

> **WORK HACK:** *Reward yourself with small wins throughout the day instead of waiting for one big success.*

2. Oxytocin: The Love Drug (a.k.a. The Warm Fuzzy Feeling)

Oxytocin makes you feel connected to others—this happens when you:

- Hug someone you love

- Bond with your dog (or a cat that tolerates you)
- Feel supported by your team at work

> **LEADERSHIP HACK:** *If you want your team to trust you, create a culture of safety. No one thrives in fear.*

3. Serotonin: The Confidence Booster (a.k.a. The "I Belong Here" Chemical)

Serotonin flows when you:

- Exercise outdoors
- Get recognition for your work
- Feel like part of a tribe

> **WORK HACK:** *Have walking meetings. Research shows that moving while talking leads to clearer thinking.*

4. Endorphins: The Painkiller (a.k.a. The "I Just Ran a Marathon and Loved It" Chemical)

Endorphins help you push through discomfort—they kick in when you:

- Exercise to the point of exhaustion
- Laugh hysterically
- Eat spicy food

> **LIFE HACK:** *If you're stressed, go do something ridiculous. Dance. Laugh. Get out of your head.*

WHY HAPPINESS ISN'T ENOUGH (AND WHY FULFILLMENT IS THE REAL GOAL)

Happiness is temporary. It's that sugar rush you get when you eat a donut, but fulfillment? That's long-term. That's the balanced diet.

- Happiness is getting a job promotion.
- Fulfillment is knowing your work makes a real impact.
- Happiness is getting married.
- Fulfillment is growing together for decades.
- Happiness is a dopamine high.
- Fulfillment is a life that aligns with your values.

> **TRUTH BOMB:** *You can be happy and still feel empty. That's why so many successful people feel miserable despite their achievements.*

AVA'S JOURNEY

I am going to take you on the journey of a young woman who might be struggling with the same kinds of things you find yourself dealing with. Age, job title, location do not matter. Ava's journey is universal.

SETTING THE STAGE: WHEN SUCCESS FEELS LIKE FAILURE

Ava had it all—or so it seemed.

At 29, she was the kind of person LinkedIn loves to worship. Founder of a hot tech startup, Stanford alum, former product prodigy at a Big Tech giant, and a *Forbes* 30 Under 30 cover star. She had 500K followers on X, 800K on Instagram, and had delivered a TED Talk that went viral—twice.

Her company? A Gen Z-loved app that somehow made scrolling more addictive, productivity more *vibes-y*, and work feel like play. Investors threw money at her like she was the next Elon, and employees whispered her name like she was a mythical unicorn CEO who cracked the secret to millennial leadership.

Her loft in San Francisco's South Beach was straight out of a tech influencer's Pinterest board—industrial-chic, overpriced, and only a short scooter ride from her office in the SOMA district. Her days were kicked off with executive staff standing meetings and packed with keynote speeches, strategy sessions, investor calls, and artfully staged coffee breaks that doubled as social media content.

From the outside, she was winning at life. Inside? She was barely holding it together.

THE STANDING MEETING THAT BROUGHT HER TO HER KNEES

Ava liked to start Mondays with momentum. Her executive team literally stood in a circle—an attempt at an *efficient, high-energy kickoff*—as each leader gave quick-fire updates on their Objectives and Key Results (OKRs) and weekly goals.

And just like every Monday, their no-BS CFO, John, spoke first.

Except this time, he didn't talk about cash flow or burn rate.

Instead, he threw his badge on the floor, grabbed his backpack, and announced:

"I quit."

Silence.

Ava barely had time to process what had just happened when Josh, their Chief Revenue Officer, sighed, stuffed his hands into his pockets, and said:

"I'm giving my notice. I'm out too."

The circle of leaders, normally buzzing with plans and action items, stood frozen in shock.

Then came the final blow.

Jenny, the Chief Success Officer, shifted uncomfortably before muttering:

"We lost another major customer. They weren't happy with the product."

And then—just to twist the knife—she looked straight at Morgan, the CTO.

Morgan, of course, rolled his eyes. The man was a genius coder, and he knew it. He had built the product. If customers weren't happy, it wasn't his problem—it was theirs for not *getting it.*

Ava barely heard the rest of the meeting. Her brain had already entered survival mode.

John was gone.

Josh was leaving.

Customers were dropping.

And her once rock-solid team looked more frustrated than inspired.

Her worst fear? Their burn rate (cost of operating the company) was too high, they were running out of money and would be in big trouble in a few months (one of reasons why John, the CFO, quit). It was all crumbling, and she had no idea how to stop it.

A WHISPER OF TRUTH

As the team dispersed in awkward silence, Ava just stood there.

Alone.

What the hell just happened?

This wasn't how things were supposed to go. She had followed all the business books, all the leadership frameworks. She had done the vision boards, the investor pitches, the team-building offsites with questionable trust-fall exercises.

And yet, here she was, watching her team implode in real time.

A few feet away, Grace, her Chief of Staff, hesitated before stepping closer.

She leaned in and whispered:

"You need to get your VIBES."

Ava blinked. "Excuse me?"

Grace smirked, patted her on the back, and walked away, leaving Ava with nothing but questions.

VIBES?

Was that some new leadership framework she had missed?

Was this a cryptic Gen Z thing? (God, she really hoped it wasn't another TikTok trend she was too old to understand.)

Or was it... something more important than all the business strategies in the world?

Ava was about to find out.

That night, Ava did what any self-respecting, burnt-out founder in crisis mode would do.

She called Waymo, let a self-driving car take her home (because making one more decision might actually break her), and crawled straight into bed.

She stared at the ceiling, still shaken from the day's events.

- Should she cry it out?
- Should she drink it out?
- Should she binge-watch Netflix until the existential dread faded?
- **Option D: All of the above.**

Within minutes, she was half-buried in a blanket fortress, a margarita in one hand, a slice of deep-dish pizza in the other, and *some random comfort show she had already seen twice* playing in the background. It wasn't exactly a productive leadership response, but at this point, who cared?

By 2 a.m., she had successfully numbed herself into oblivion, momentarily convinced that her company wasn't on the verge of collapse and her career wasn't unraveling at high speed.

By 2:30 AM, she was passed out.

THE LITTLE BLACK BOX THAT CHANGED EVERYTHING

The next morning, the doorbell rang.

Ava groaned. What fresh hell is this?

She shuffled to the door—her mascara smudged, hair looking like it had survived a minor electrical fire—and yanked it open.

No one was there.

Just a little black box.

On the front: Her name. No sender. No return address.

Still groggy, she picked it up and carried it inside. She expected it to be some expensive, unnecessary PR package from a brand trying to collaborate.

She opened the box.

Inside was a handwritten note, a little brass pocket compass and an airline ticket to Marrakech—departing in three hours.

She frowned, flipping over the note.

"You need to find VIBES. Start with Marrakech."

Her stomach dropped.

What. The. Actual. Hell.

Who sent this?

How did they know she was falling apart?

And—wait. Marrakech? As in, *Morocco*?

Ava glanced at the clock. She had exactly 20 minutes to decide.

Sit in her loft, spiral into existential doom, and rewatch *Gossip Girl* for the thirty-fourth time?

Or get on a plane to a mystery adventure she didn't ask for?

She stared at the tickets.

Then at the pizza box from last night.

Then back to the tickets.

Screw it.

She grabbed a bag and started packing.

THE TRIP TO NOWHERE?

Ava was not in the mood for adventure.

Her journey had consisted of:

1. A middle seat on a packed flight to Amsterdam, wedged between a chatty tech bro explaining *crypto arbitrage* and a woman who apparently had a deep, personal vendetta against deodorant.

2. A back-row seat by the rear bathrooms on the second leg to Morocco, where she got to experience every flush like a personal soundtrack to her suffering and a rush of foul bathroom stench.

3. A brutal hangover that, combined with airplane food, had made her question every decision she had ever made.

By the time she landed in Marrakech, she was over it.

Wasn't this supposed to be a luxury leadership retreat? Maybe a week at the Four Seasons, where she would sit through workshops with other burned-out CEOs and learn "10 Hacks to Lead with Impact" while sipping mint tea by the pool?

Instead, she got blinding afternoon sunlight, suffocating dry heat, and an airport full of people who actually seemed to know why they were here.

Ava? She had no clue.

PART 1

CHAPTER 1

V — VALUES & BELIEFS

The Compass That Guides You

TRUST ISSUES & OLD DIESEL ENGINES

After clearing immigration and collecting her suitcase, she spotted a man holding a white sheet of paper with her name on it.

The first thought that crossed her mind—Should I trust this guy?

The man, dressed in a loose-fitting djellaba, gave her a polite nod.

"Miss Aaava?" he asked.

She hesitated, then nodded.

He grabbed her bag and led her to an old Mercedes, the kind that looked like it had survived a war, a flood, and several major life crises.

The car smelled exactly like her grandpa's truck—a potent mix of old diesel fuel and leather.

She climbed in and instantly regretted it.

No air conditioning. The hot wind blew in through the open windows, carrying the scent of spices, dust, and sweat. Within minutes, she had at least two layers of perspiration and was mentally preparing her eulogy.

"Where are we going?" she asked, already dreading the answer.

The driver, gripping the wheel with the casual confidence of someone who had seen things, glanced at her in the rearview mirror.

"We go to Abdi."

Ava squinted. "Where is Abdi?"

The driver grinned. "Abdi is person."

Oh. Well. That cleared up exactly nothing.

REALITY SETS IN

As they left the city, Ava watched the buildings fade into open desert, the last traces of streetlights disappearing in the distance.

Okay, so definitely not the Four Seasons.

The diesel engine rumbled on, eating up mile after mile of empty road.

No signs.

No people.

No Wi-Fi.

Ava felt vulnerable for the first time since her first boyfriend dumped her via text message.

She clutched her phone, zero bars, and briefly considered the possibility that she was being kidnapped. Was this how tech founders went missing? She imagined the headlines:

Startup CEO Leaves for Leadership Retreat, Ends Up in Unknown Desert.

Her only company was the low hum of the engine, the dry heat sticking to her skin, and the heavy, sinking realization she had no idea where the hell she was going.

For the first time in a long time, Ava wasn't in control.

And that terrified her.

The old, beaten leather backseats of the diesel Mercedes hugged Ava tightly, as if they knew she needed comfort. Maybe she was just so exhausted that even a questionable, slightly sticky backseat felt like a five-star mattress.

Either way, she passed out immediately.

And for the first time in 48 hours, she slept deeply.

LOST IN THE DARK

A gentle tap on her shoulder woke her.

Ava blinked awake, but strangely, she wasn't startled. That nap? Better than melatonin, better than a weighted blanket, better than all the overpriced meditation apps she had downloaded and never used.

The driver, unbothered as ever, simply pointed into the pitch-black abyss outside.

"Abdi."

ABDI, THE MYSTERIOUS MAN

Ava rubbed her eyes and looked around.

They had stopped on the side of a desert road that barely existed. No signs. No buildings. Just sand. So much sand.

Before she could ask questions, the driver unloaded her bags, placed them neatly on the ground, gave her a small nod, and climbed back into his trusty diesel-powered chariot of doom.

Ava stood frozen, watching as the old Mercedes rumbled away, its distinctive diesel growl fading into the distance.

This had to be a mistake.

This had to be a joke.

She turned in circles, straining to see something—anything—through the darkness. The only light came from the stars, blazing across the sky like someone had dumped an entire galaxy's worth of glitter overhead.

She took a deep breath and a tentative step forward. Her feet sank into the warm desert sand.

Still no Abdi.

Still no sign of civilization.

Ava felt her chest tighten.

She spun around. The Mercedes was a tiny dot on the horizon now.

"WAIT!" she shouted, running after it, arms flailing like a madwoman.

"This has gotta be a mistake! WAIT!"

She took two big steps—then face-planted into the sand.

Mouth full of desert.

Excellent. Now she was lost AND eating sand.

ABDI APPEARS

A strong, calloused hand reached down and gently lifted her to her feet.

Ava coughed, spitting out what felt like half of Morocco, and looked up.

There, standing in front of her, was a man with leathery sun-kissed skin, a flowing white man-dress, and a matching turban wrapped around his head. His sandals were worn, but sturdy. He looked both ancient and age-less at the same time.

His eyes? Calm. Kind. Unshaken.

And then, in the most casual, no-big-deal tone, he said:

"I am Abdi."

Ava wiped sand from her face, still unsure if this was a dream, a hallucina-tion, or the beginning of a very bad life choice.

Behind him, two camels stood patiently, chewing and staring at her like she was the least impressive thing they'd seen all day.

Abdi tilted his head toward the horizon, where the first hints of sunrise painted the sky in soft golds and pinks.

He extended a hand. "We go."

Ava turned, looking out at the endless ocean of sand ahead.

No hotel. No phone signal. No exit strategy. Just the desert.

And the journey that was about to begin.

NOTHING BUT DESERT

Ava had many regrets in life—ordering sushi from gas stations, dating a guy who thought crypto was a personality, trusting her CFO *not* to quit in the middle of a meeting—but agreeing to travel across the desert on a camel with a mysterious man named Abdi was quickly rising to the top of that list.

It had been two days in the unforgiving Moroccan sun, and Ava was convinced she was actually melting.

Her once-sleek San Francisco wardrobe was now a sand-stained, sweat-soaked mess. Her face felt like beef jerky, her legs were sore in places she didn't know existed, and her camel? An unbothered, grumpy creature that had decided, multiple times, that stopping mid-stride to chew something invisible was more important than moving forward.

Abdi, on the other hand? Completely unfazed.

He sat atop his camel with the calm composure of a man who had conquered both nature and inner peace.

Ava hated him for it.

She groaned. "Abdi, are we even going the right way?"

Without looking back, he simply pointed to the sky.

"The stars will guide us," he said.

Ava squinted. "It's daytime."

Abdi just smiled.

And then—disaster struck.

AVA VS. THE SNAKE

Ava wasn't sure if she blacked out from heat exhaustion or dehydration, but one moment she was on her camel, and the next—

She was face-first in the sand.

"Ugh," she groaned, spitting out a mouthful of desert for the second time in 48 hours.

She turned over and sat up, her body aching, her head spinning.

And then, she saw it.

A deadly looking snake, its scales gleaming under the scorching sun, hissing directly at her.

Ava froze.

"Abdi," she whispered. "I don't want to alarm you, but I'm about to die."

Abdi, ever patient, walked over like this was just another Tuesday.

Without a word, he bent down, grabbed the snake behind its head with terrifying ease, pulled out a knife, and in one swift motion—SWIPE.

The head dropped to the sand.

Ava gasped. "Oh my god."

Abdi held up the rest of the snake.

"Dinner," he said, completely serious.

Ava blinked. "I was really hoping for… I don't know… something from a menu?"

THE CAMPFIRE STORY: THE TEST OF THE DESERT

That night, under the vast Moroccan sky, Ava and Abdi sat by the fire, their meal of snake-which-tastes-like-chicken now reduced to bones. The embers glowed, casting dancing shadows on the sand, while above them, the universe spilled itself out in stars—brighter, more infinite than anything Ava had ever seen back in San Francisco.

Abdi leaned back, staring at the sky as if reading an old familiar book. Then, in his usual unhurried way, he spoke.

"When I turned 12, my father brought me here. Just like his father before him, and his father before that."

Ava, already half-lulled into the rhythm of the desert, raised an eyebrow. "A generational field trip? Sounds ... intense."

Abdi chuckled. "Intense, yes. Necessary? Also, yes." He stirred the fire with a stick, watching the sparks float into the night like tiny shooting stars.

"On the second night, my father passed down to me words of wisdom that spanned generations. He said, 'There are as many stars in the sky as there are grains of sand in the desert. My father and his father's ashes are scattered into the desert. Their spirits surround us.' The desert is alive. It speaks. And if you listen closely, it will guide you.'"

Ava glanced at the vast emptiness around them, skeptical. "I don't hear much except the wind."

Abdi nodded. "Most people don't. Because most people don't listen."

The fire crackled, as if agreeing with him.

THE TEST OF THE DESERT

Abdi continued.

"My father told me, 'When you are lost, do not panic. Do not run. Do not fight. You will not win against the desert. Instead, you must fall back on what is inside you—your values, your beliefs. They will be your guide when all else is lost.'"

Ava wrapped her arms around her knees, feeling the desert's chill creeping in.

"That night, I fell asleep. And when I woke up, the fire was out."

Ava frowned. "And let me guess—your dad was gone?"

Abdi smiled. "Exactly, I was alone. Just like you were when the car dropped you off that night."

Ava exhaled slowly.

She had felt that fear—that moment of being untethered—unsure if she should run or freeze.

"I checked my little bag," Abdi said. "My father had left me two days' worth of water and five medjool dates. I knew we had traveled for two days, so I believed that if I retraced our steps, I would find my way back in that time."

Ava nodded. Smart.

"But by the end of day two, my water was gone."

Ava's stomach tightened.

"By day three, I was still lost."

She swallowed. "Okay … now that's terrifying."

Abdi nodded. "I ate one date. Chewed the seed for every last bit of energy. By day four, I ate my last date. Still, I walked."

Ava's heart started racing. "And you weren't scared?"

Abdi shook his head. "I remembered what my father told me—do not panic. Do not run. Trust the desert, and trust yourself."

Ava shivered, not from the cold, but from the weight of the story.

"I had nothing left but my beliefs," Abdi said. "I believed the desert would not take me. It would take care of me."

Ava wanted to question that logic. But deep down, she knew exactly what he meant.

"That's when I saw a desert beetle."

Ava's nose scrunched. "Please don't tell me you—"

"I ate it."

Ava groaned. "Of course you did."

Abdi grimaced. "And you know what? It gave me energy. Energy I didn't know I had. And that energy... led me in the right direction."

He looked toward the fire. "A few hours later, I saw my father."

Ava let out a breath.

"He hugged me. Told me he was proud. He knew I would find my way if I believed in what I had inside me."

Silence.

Ava stared at the burning embers, her mind pulling at something deep inside her.

She had spent her entire life chasing external validation—what investors thought, what social media thought, what her team thought.

She had never asked herself what she thought.

She had never written down her values, let alone reviewed them like a compass to guide her.

Had she even been following the right stars?

She exhaled slowly. "And now you do that, seek answers in the stars? Every night?"

Abdi nodded. "I review them like affirmations. Every night before I go to sleep."

Ava swallowed. She had so many questions.

But her eyes grew heavy.

A FAMILIAR TEST

The desert air wrapped around her like a heavy blanket, and soon, Ava drifted into sleep.

When she opened her eyes, the fire was out.

She sat up quickly.

Her heart dropped.

Abdi was gone.

The camels? Gone.

The footprints? Already erased by the shifting sands.

Panic surged up her throat.

No. No. No.

She spun around. The vast desert stretched out in every direction, empty, silent, and indifferent to her crisis.

She was completely alone.

LOST—AGAIN

Ava jumped to her feet, her breath shallow.

She was back in tech CEO mode now—running through worst-case scenarios like an algorithm crunching data.

1. She had no supplies.

2. She had no map.

3. She had no idea where Abdi went.

She clenched her fists. Was this another test?

Her brain screamed, "DO SOMETHING!"

Then, her grandfather's voice echoed in her memory.

"Keep your head straight and follow your northern stars."

She also remembered what Abdi's father said about the desert: "Do not panic. Do not run. Trust the desert, and trust yourself."

Her pulse slowed.

She reached into her pocket.

Her fingers closed around something cool and familiar.

The brass pocket compass.

The same one from the mysterious black box that started this whole journey.

She flipped it open.

The needle pointed north.

She took a deep breath, squared her shoulders, and started walking.

"Do not panic. Do not run. Trust the desert, and trust yourself."

A NEW BEGINNING

Hours passed.

The sun blazed overhead.

Ava's legs trembled. Her body screamed for rest.

Night fell and all she had was the desert and her thoughts as she sat alone in the sand. What are my values? She fell asleep.

The next morning, she woke up, her stomach growl echoing in her body. She had two days of water and had drunk almost all of it. She didn't have any food and felt weak. Suddenly, she saw a desert beetle running across the sand and burrowing itself under the sand to keep cool from the burning sun. Ava thought to herself, *there is no way I will eat an insect, ever!* She threw her arms up, chased the beetle, grabbed it and imagining it was an exotic sushi roll, shoved it into her mouth. She chewed on it with her mouth open and swallowed. She then saw another beetle and did the same. She took a small sip of water to wash it down.

Maybe it was physical or psychological or both, but she felt new energy surging through her body.

At night, she laid down on her back and stared at the stars. She thought more about her values. "What do I value in life, what are my beliefs, what drives me, what is my purpose in life, what is my true north?" She took out her pocket notebook and wrote:

- **Integrity:** Doing what's right, even when no one is watching.
- **Curiosity:** Always seeking to learn and grow.
- **Connection:** Forging meaningful relationships.
- **Courage:** Taking action despite fear.
- **Joy:** Not just existing, but truly living.

The next morning, she started walking and followed the needle on the compass pointing north. She had run out of water and felt her muscles tensing up with dehydration. She couldn't find any more beetles to feed on. Her feet felt like lead.

In the late afternoon, just as she thought she couldn't take another step, she fell on her back and stared up at the sky. Ava was exhausted and having an out-of-body experience, her eyes half open, somewhere in between a state of unconsciousness and somewhere else that she'd never been before.

A hand tapped her shoulder gently.

She gasped and sat up.

Abdi.

Standing there, his eyes knowing, his presence steady.

Ava exhaled, half in relief, half in awe.

She stared at him. "Did you find me? Or did I find you?"

Abdi just smiled.

BACK TO CIVILIZATION & THE NEXT JOURNEY

In the distance, trees appeared.

And beyond them? Buildings.

They had reached the edge of Marrakech.

As the old diesel Mercedes appeared from nowhere, Ava felt a strange mix of relief and reluctance.

Abdi helped her down from the camel.

For a moment, she just looked at him.

And then—without overthinking it—she hugged him.

"Thank you, Abdi. You helped me find my true north."

Abdi nodded. "The journey is never over."

She climbed into the car.

On the seat? Another mysterious black box.

She opened it.

Inside was a handwritten note:

"You found V – Values & Beliefs. Go to Japan."

Next to it was a delicate Japanese teacup.

And a ticket to Kyoto.

Ava smiled.

The journey goes on.

PRACTICAL EXERCISES TO DO:

1. **The Written Compass:** Write down five core values that define you. Then, for each one, write an action that aligns with that value. Reflect on how often you actually live by them. (Note from the author: Pablo Picasso once famously said, *"Good artists copy; great artists steal."* The same applies to values. It's perfectly fine to take inspiration from Ava's values—or even "steal" them—as a starting point for defining your own. Values aren't meant to be hoarded; they evolve, adapt, and influence. Some people find their values through personal experiences, while others draw from religious or philosophical beliefs. However you shape them, what matters most is that they truly guide your decisions, actions, and the culture you build.)

    EXAMPLE: *Let's take one of Ava's core values:* **Courage**

    ACTION: *I speak up in meetings, even when my ideas might be unpopular.*

    REFLECTION: *I do this about 60% of the time—but I want to raise that to 90%. I've noticed when I don't speak up, I leave feeling regretful and out of alignment with myself.*

2. **The Decision Filter:** Before making a decision—personal or professional—ask: Does this align with my core values? If not, why am I considering it?

3. **The Desert Test:** Imagine you lost everything—job, money, status. What remains important to you? That's your true compass.

UNCONVENTIONAL EXERCISES:

1. **The Stranger's Perspective:** Ask three people who know you well to describe your values in three words. Compare this to what you think your values are. Are they aligned or is there a gap?

2. **The 24-Hour Authenticity Challenge:** For an entire day, make every decision based 100% on your values. Say no to anything that doesn't align. See how it feels.

3. **The "Last Day Alive" Test:** Imagine this is your last day on earth. What would you do? What matters most? Those are your core values in action.

5 PRACTICAL TOOLS FOR VALUES & BELIEFS:

1. **Define Your Personal & Work Values Separately:** Then Merge Them – See if they align. If they don't, you're living in conflict.

2. **Use Your Values as a Hiring & Leadership Filter:** Great leaders hire for values, not just skills. Skills can be taught; values are ingrained.

3. **Review Your Values Like Affirmations:** Just like Abdi did. Every night, reflect on how you honored your values that day.

4. **Make a "Non-Negotiables" List:** What will you never compromise on in life and work? Write it down. Stick to it.

5. **When Lost, Follow Your Compass:** If confused, revisit your values. They always point north.

NEUROSCIENCE FACTS ON VALUES & BELIEFS:

- **The Prefrontal Cortex & Decision-Making:** The prefrontal cortex (the brain's CEO) is responsible for long-term thinking and decision-making—it thrives when aligned with clear values.

- **The Amygdala & Fear of Change:** Your amygdala (the emotional center) resists change, but when values are reinforced through action, neural pathways strengthen, making value-based decision making easier over time.

- **Cognitive Dissonance & Stress:** When you act against your values, your brain experiences cognitive dissonance—a stress response. Living by your values reduces mental tension and increases fulfillment.

CONCLUSION & TAKEAWAYS:

→ **Values aren't just words;** they are the GPS of life.

→ **When you feel lost, realign with your values**—they will always show you the way.

→ **Strong values create strong leadership.** Strong leadership creates a strong culture.

CHAPTER 2:

I — INTERACTION & COMMUNICATION

The Language of Connection

THE FLIGHT TO KYOTO & A STRANGER'S SILENCE

Ava sat in yet another back-row airplane seat, wedged between a snoring businessman and a college student who had taken his shoes off his ripe feet.

She stared at the Japanese teacup she had found in the black box.

Why a teacup?

The note had been clear: Go to Japan. You found Values & Beliefs—now find Interaction & Communication.

Which, frankly, felt a little insulting because Ava was pretty sure she already knew how to communicate.

She had given TED Talks, pitched VCs, built an online following of nearly a million people. If anything, talking was her strongest skill.

But now? Sitting alone, watching the flight map inch its way toward Kyoto, she wondered—was she actually good at communication?

Or was she just good at talking?

THE SILENT TEA HOUSE

Ava had expected Kyoto to be bustling, like Tokyo, with neon signs and fast-paced energy. Instead, it was quiet—serene in a way that felt almost unnatural to her Silicon Valley-wired brain.

An old man holding a white paper with her name written on it met her at the airport and guided her to his parked car.

The sun was just beginning to stretch its golden arms across the Kyoto skyline when Ava stepped outside Kansai International Airport. Her jet-lagged body moved slowly, but her eyes were wide open, soaking in the clean lines, efficient signage, and surreal sense of order that only Japan could offer.

A black Toyota Crown Royal—a symbol of understated elegance and quiet power—glided to a soft stop in front of her. The paint gleamed like polished obsidian. The driver stepped out with deliberate grace. He was an older man, perhaps in his late sixties, with neatly combed silver hair and a navy chauffeur's cap perched just so. His uniform was spotless, his white gloves pristine, and his posture perfect.

He bowed deeply, his expression calm and courteous. Ava, startled by the warmth and formality of the gesture, quickly returned the bow, though her form was a little more yoga-stretch than cultural grace. "Arigatou gozaimasu," she said, hoping her Duolingo binge had paid off.

The driver nodded approvingly, opened the rear door with a soft flourish, and gestured for her to enter. The inside of the Crown Royal was immaculate. It smelled faintly of cherry blossoms and cedar—clean, calming, intentional. A white lace doily covered the headrest, and a tiny ceramic cat with a raised paw waved from the dashboard.

As they pulled away from the airport, Ava noticed how smooth the ride was—almost meditative. There was no honking, no swerving, no chaos. The driver guided the vehicle with the steady hands of someone who saw driving not as a job but as a craft.

They didn't speak much, but the silence wasn't awkward. It was respectful. In between sips of complimentary green tea from a chilled bottle he had offered, Ava stared out the window, watching the city shift from rural quiet to urban rhythm. Neon signs began to appear, tucked between ancient temples and minimalist architecture.

This wasn't just a car ride. It was her first lesson in Japanese culture: humility, hospitality, and harmony in nature.

And though the driver was simply a transport guide, he felt like her first teacher.

As they approached the monastery on the outskirts of the city above the Gion district, where she would soon meet her next mentor—Kenji—Ava's heart began to shift gears. The silence outside mirrored the stillness inside her. She didn't know what she was driving toward exactly—but she knew the journey had truly begun.

Inside, a man in traditional robes greeted her with a slight bow.

He led her to a low wooden table, placed a single teacup in front of her, and then—

He said nothing.

Ava stared at him.

He stared back, expression unreadable.

She cleared her throat. "Uh… hi?"

No response.

Ava shifted in her seat. Maybe he didn't speak English?

"Tea?" she asked, trying again.

Still nothing.

Was this… was this the exercise? Uncomfortable silence until she lost her mind?

After what felt like an eternity, the man—still silent—began making tea with deliberate, careful movements.

Ava watched, slightly mesmerized as he heated the water, measured the leaves, and poured with the kind of patience she had never once applied to anything in her life.

No rushing. No unnecessary movements. Just precision and presence.

Finally, he pushed the cup toward her.

She hesitated before picking it up and taking a sip.

Warm. Earthy. Unlike anything she had ever tasted before.

The silence continued.

She fidgeted. Should she fill the silence?

Should she ask a question? Crack a joke?

And then—

She realized something.

She didn't need to talk.

For the first time in her life, she let silence be silence.

THE ART OF LISTENING

After what felt like forever, the man finally spoke.

"You listen only to respond."

Ava blinked. *Excuse me?*

He continued, "But true communication is when you listen to understand."

Oh.

Oh.

Ava thought about her life. Her meetings. Her team.

She always had a rebuttal ready. A next point. A counter-argument.

Even when someone else was talking, she was already preparing what to say next.

She had been hearing—but she hadn't really been listening.

True communication is when you listen to understand.

The man refilled her tea.

"The space between words is where meaning lives."

Ava swallowed.

She had spent her whole career filling the space with more words. More pitches. More convincing.

Maybe that was why her team had started falling apart.

She had been talking "at" them. Not "with" them.

At night, Ava sat in a meditative pose and thought about her interactions with Kenji. She repeated her five values as affirmations (Integrity, Curiosity, Connection, Courage, and Joy) and went to bed on the Japanese-style futon on the hard bamboo floor.

LEARNING THE POWER OF SILENCE

Ava had never spent this much time in silence before.

Her first day with Kenji had been unsettling. The deliberate tea ritual, the long stretches of wordless interaction, the way he let her sit in her own discomfort—it was a lot.

But something shifted overnight.

When she woke up the next morning in the small tatami-style room provided by the teahouse, she felt calmer than she had in years.

No buzzing phone.

No morning emails.

No back-to-back investor meetings.

Just the slow, deliberate rhythm of Kyoto waking up.

Kenji greeted her with a nod but, once again, said nothing.

This time, Ava didn't fill the silence.

She simply followed as he led her outside, away from the teahouse, into the lush, green embrace of a nearby bamboo forest leading path to Higashiyama Mountains.

THE SOUND OF NATURE & THE WEIGHT OF WORDS

The morning air was crisp, carrying the scent of pine and fresh earth.

They walked in silence.

At first, Ava's mind raced. Was this another test? Were they going somewhere? Was she supposed to be learning something?

Then—she noticed.

The whisper of the wind through the bamboo stalks.

The soft crunch of her footsteps against the dirt path.

The distant call of a bird she couldn't name.

For the first time, she was fully present.

They reached a modest wooden teahouse perched high on the mountainside, nestled beside a still pond that mirrored the sky like polished glass. The clearing, unusually flat for its altitude, was encircled by thick, vibrant greenery that whispered with the breeze. Ava followed Kenji through a tiny sliding door—no taller than a doggie door—into what looked like a centuries-old wooden hut, humble yet timeless.

Inside, the scent of cedar and ash lingered in the air. Kenji moved with deliberate calm, settling onto a raised platform where he began arranging a few pieces of charcoal in an aged steel hibachi with the care of a man performing a ritual. He motioned silently for Ava to take her place on a small wooden bench across from him.

They sat there for a long time.

Then, with quiet precision, Kenji placed a cast iron tetsubin atop the glowing coals, the soft clink of metal against metal echoing in the stillness. He opened a delicate porcelain container and, using a slender bamboo spoon—chakusha—scooped two perfect portions of vibrant green matcha.

He placed the powder into a handcrafted chawan and added just enough boiling water from the kettle. With a bamboo whisk—chasen—he stirred in smooth, rhythmic strokes until the tea frothed into a silky emerald foam.

Kenji bowed slightly and extended the chawan to Ava with both hands. She accepted it reverently, brought it to her lips, and took a slow sip. The matcha was earthy, rich, and alive—like drinking the mountain itself.

THE STORY OF THE SAMURAI & THE MONK

"A long time ago," Kenji began, "a powerful samurai came to a Zen monk seeking wisdom."

Ava sat up straighter. A story.

"The samurai was known for his strength, his skill in battle. But he was also known for his anger. His words were sharp, like his sword, and he used them without care. He spoke often but never listened. He was feared but not respected."

Ava's fingers tightened around the edge of her bench. She knew a lot of CEOs like that.

Kenji continued, "The samurai asked the monk, 'Teach me the secret to wisdom. I want to understand the way of Zen.'

The monk simply nodded and began making tea.

The samurai grew impatient. He demanded answers. 'Why won't you speak?'

Still, the monk remained silent.

Then—he began pouring sencha tea into the samurai's cup.

He poured, and poured—until the tea spilled over, running across the table.

'What are you doing?' the samurai yelled. 'The cup is full!'

The monk finally spoke. 'Yes,' he said. 'And so is your mind. You are so full of your own thoughts, your own voice, that there is no room for wisdom. If you wish to learn, you must first empty your cup.'"

Kenji turned to Ava. "What do you think the samurai did next?"

Ava thought for a moment. "Did he listen?"

Kenji nodded. "He listened."

Ava let out a slow breath.

Empty the cup.

How many times had she walked into meetings already convinced she knew the answer?

How many conversations had she led without actually hearing what others were saying?

COMMUNICATING WITH INTENTION & POSITIVE ENERGY

Once they stepped out of the wooden hut, Kenji turned back to the trees.

"The wind does not shout," he said. "Yet it moves the trees."

Ava frowned. "Meaning?"

Kenji smiled. "True leadership does not come from who speaks the loudest. It comes from the one who listens, who moves people not with force, but with energy."

He picked up a small rock and tossed it into the nearby pond. Ripples spread outward, reaching the edges before disappearing.

"Every word you speak is like this rock," he said. "It creates an effect. It moves others. But if you throw without thinking, you create only chaos."

Ava thought about the last few months at her company.

The way John, her CFO, had walked out.

The way Josh, the CRO, had given his notice.

The way her leadership team looked at her, frustrated, unheard.

She spoke often. But had she spoken with intention?

Had she listened before speaking?

True leadership does not come from who speaks the loudest.

Had she been throwing rocks without thinking about the ripples?

Kenji made her another cup of tea. "Words, like tea, should be poured carefully. Measured. With purpose."

Ava picked up her cup.

She didn't speak.

She just nodded.

She was starting to understand.

THE WALK TO NOWHERE

The next morning, Kenji took her on another walk. This time, they left the village and wandered through Kyoto's quiet winding streets in the Gion district.

Ava didn't ask where they were going.

She simply walked, listening to the world around her.

The rustling leaves.

The murmurs of shopkeepers opening their stores.

The soft hum of distant traffic.

After nearly an hour, she stopped.

She turned to Kenji. "Are we lost?"

Kenji simply smiled. "Are we?"

Ava hesitated, then looked back.

She had no idea how to get back to the teahouse.

But she also wasn't panicking.

She had been too focused on the journey.

Kenji nodded, as if reading her thoughts. "When you listen, you will always find your way."

Ava took a deep breath.

She wasn't just listening to the world around her anymore.

She was listening to herself.

A FAMILIAR BLACK BOX

By the time they returned to the teahouse, a familiar sight awaited her.

Another black box.

She opened it.

Inside— A small river stone.

A handwritten note: "You found I – Interaction & Communication. Go to Thailand."

And—of course—another plane ticket.

Ava sighed, but this time, she smiled.

Ava and Kenji bowed to each other. She leapt forward and gave him a tight hug. He was surprised but smiled and went to his regular meditation spot.

She had entered Kyoto thinking she already knew everything about communication.

Now?

She was leaving with a quiet mind, an empty cup, and a whole new understanding.

The journey goes on.

PRACTICAL EXERCISES TO DO:

1. **The 3-Second Rule:** When listening, pause for 3 seconds after the other person finishes speaking before responding. It forces you to truly process their words.

2. **Silence Challenge:** Spend one hour in total silence. Observe how much your mind wants to fill the space. This builds comfort in listening and observing.

3. **Body Language Mirror:** Stand in front of a mirror and observe your posture, eye contact, and expression when speaking. Non-verbal cues are 55% of communication.

3 UNCONVENTIONAL EXERCISES:

1. **Silent Meetings:** Have a 30-minute team meeting where no one speaks—all communication must happen via writing (on whiteboards, chat apps, or sticky notes). Observe how people's messages change when they have to be intentional.

2. **The Five-Minute Wait:** The next time you feel the urge to correct, defend, or respond, wait five minutes before saying anything. Train yourself to listen and process before reacting.

3. **The Forced Empathy Experiment:** Pick someone you don't like or find difficult to work with. Spend a day pretending you are them—what do they care about? What's their struggle? This rewires how you engage with difficult people.

5 PRACTICAL TOOLS FOR INTERACTION & COMMUNICATION:

1. **Listen to Understand, Not to Respond:** True communication is about hearing, not waiting for your turn to talk.

2. **Master the Power of the Pause:** Pausing before responding makes your words more intentional and impactful.

3. **Clarify Before Assuming:** Ask "What I'm hearing is…" to avoid miscommunication.

4. **Use Silence as a Leadership Tool:** Silence creates space for deeper conversation and trust.

5. **Practice the Rule of 3:** If something is important, say it three different ways-verbally, visually, and emotionally.

NEUROSCIENCE FACTS ON COMMUNICATION:

- **Mirror Neurons & Connection:** When we deeply listen, our mirror neurons activate, increasing **empathy and connection.**

- **The Power of a 7-Second Pause:** Studies show a 7-second pause before responding boosts trust and perception of intelligence.

- **Oxytocin & Storytelling:** When you share personal stories, your brain releases oxytocin, making you more relatable and influential.

CONCLUSION & TAKEAWAYS:

→ **The best communicators don't talk more.** They listen better.

→ **Silence is not empty;** it's full of meaning.

→ **Words create reality**—use them wisely.

CHAPTER 3

B — BEHAVIORS & RITUALS

Small Actions, Big Impact

WELCOME TO THE UNKNOWN

Ava had been to Thailand before—but on a luxury work retreat, where she spent most of the time at a five-star resort pretending to be relaxed while secretly answering emails.

This time? Very different.

Her bumpy flight, middle seat, the sweaty smells, and the thick air in the airplane with the sub-par air conditioning didn't bother her.

Her arrival in Bangkok was a humid slap to the face. The air smelled of lemongrass, grilled meat, and the faint suggestion of exhaust fumes. The city was alive—motorbikes darting through traffic, street vendors flipping sizzling woks, monks in saffron robes weaving through the chaos with supernatural calm.

But she wasn't here to stay in Bangkok.

The note in the familiar black box had been clear:

"Go to Chiang Mai. Find Bodhi."

THE JOURNEY TO THE JUNGLE

The driver who picked Ava up at the Chiang Mai airport looked like he had been personally sent by time itself. He had yet another sheet of white paper with Ava's name handwritten on it.

His face was carved with deep lines, his eyes steady and knowing, as if he had been driving this route since before cars existed. He didn't say much— just handed her a bottle of water, threw her bag into the back of an ancient, rust-colored Toyota Hilux truck that looked like it had survived at least three monsoon seasons, a flood, and possibly a revolution.

The truck smelled of sun-warmed leather, gasoline, and faint traces of betel nut.

As they pulled away from the city, the familiar sounds of motorbikes and street vendors along with the smoggy smell faded. Soon, the roads narrowed, the concrete turned to packed dirt, and civilization unraveled into a lush, green jungle that seemed to breathe around her.

The air grew thick and humid, wrapping around her like a warm blanket. The scent of fresh rain, damp earth, and blooming frangipani filled her lungs.

The only sounds were the steady hum of the engine, the occasional chirp of unseen insects, and the rhythmic clank of something loose in the truck bed rattling with every bump.

Ava gripped the seat tightly as the truck swerved around sharp bends, climbing higher and higher into the hills.

The driver said nothing for the first hour.

Then, as they crossed a wooden bridge over a narrow river, he finally spoke.

"Go to meet Bodhi."

Ava turned to him, waiting for more.

Nothing.

She sighed and leaned back, watching the jungle swallow the road ahead.

She was heading into the unknown. Again.

THE MAN WHO SAID NOTHING

By the time the truck finally lurched to a stop, Ava felt lightheaded from the heat and the endless curves of the jungle road.

The driver pointed toward a narrow path disappearing into the thick trees.

"Go."

Ava wiped the sweat from her forehead. "Go where?"

He simply smiled. "Bodhi waits."

She glanced down the shaded, winding path. It looked both peaceful and slightly ominous—like something out of a fable where people go in and never come out.

With no choice but forward, she slung her backpack over her shoulder and started walking.

The jungle was alive, and it felt like it had swallowed her.

The sound of cicadas buzzed in waves, birds called to each other, and the thick canopy above filtered the sun into patches of gold on the dirt path. The deeper she went, the cooler the air became, rich with the scent of moist earth, old wood, and something floral she couldn't quite place.

After what felt like an eternity, the path opened into a small clearing.

A single wooden hut stood raised against the backdrop of the towering green hills.

And there, sitting cross-legged in the shade, was a man. It must have been Bodhi.

He was older than she expected, his hair silver and his skin weathered by the sun. He wore loose linen clothing, and in his hands, he held a small knife, slowly peeling a mango.

He didn't greet her.

He didn't acknowledge her presence at all.

He simply peeled the mango, slice by careful slice.

Ava cleared her throat. "Uh … are you Bodhi?"

No response.

She shifted on her feet. "I was sent here to learn. Do you… want me to do something?"

THE MANGO LESSON

Bodhi led Ava into the small hut. Inside, it was minimal but clean—just a wooden table, a few clay pots, and a small, open-air kitchen area where a single mango rested on a banana leaf.

Bodhi picked up the mango and handed it to Ava.

"Eat."

Ava hesitated. She had eaten mango before, but never one that looked this perfectly ripe, almost glowing in the dim light of the hut.

She took a bite.

Instantly, the flavor exploded in her mouth—juicy, sweet, and richer than any mango she had ever tasted. The kind of fruit that made you want to close your eyes and savor every second.

"Wow," she mumbled between bites.

Bodhi watched her for a moment, then said, "That mango is like your mind."

Ava paused mid-chew. "My mind is a mango?"

Bodhi ignored her sarcasm. "When the mango is young, it is hard, bitter, and impatient. If you try to eat it too soon, you ruin the experience. But if you wait—if you let it grow, ripen, and take its time—it becomes something worth savoring."

Ava swallowed. "So … you're saying I've been living my life like an unripe mango?"

Bodhi smiled. "More like one that was plucked too early and left in the back of a refrigerator, trying to ripen under artificial light."

Ouch.

THE ROOM (OR LACK THEREOF)

Bodhi gestured to the corner of the hut, where there was a thin blanket neatly folded on the floor and a small pillow tucked into the corner.

"That's your room."

Ava stared at the spot, then at Bodhi.

"You mean… that's where I put my stuff?"

Bodhi raised an eyebrow. "No. That's where you sleep."

She opened her mouth to protest—surely, there was a guesthouse, a cot, a hammock, something— but then she caught herself. She was here to learn. To change.

She dropped her bag next to the blanket. "Perfect."

Bodhi nodded approvingly.

NIGHT FALLS IN THE JUNGLE

As night fell, the jungle came alive.

The sounds she had barely noticed during the day now boomed like a surround-sound nature documentary. Frogs croaked in a deep, almost mechanical rhythm. Insects chirped and buzzed in an unpredictable symphony. Somewhere in the distance, a monkey shrieked like it had just received bad news.

It felt like she had been dropped into a scene from a *Rambo* movie, complete with lush greenery, flickering shadows, and a feeling that something could be watching from the trees.

Ava wrapped herself in the blanket, which felt as thin as a napkin, and curled up on the hard wooden floor. The pillow was barely thicker than a folded T-shirt, but she reminded herself—this was part of the experience.

She took a deep breath and closed her eyes.

"Integrity. Curiosity. Connection. Courage. Joy."

She whispered her five values into the darkness. Then, she repeated her affirmations:

"I am strong. I am open. I am learning. I trust myself. I belong here."

The jungle outside hummed and pulsed, a living, breathing force.

Despite the discomfort, despite the uncertainty, Ava smiled.

She was exactly where she needed to be.

THE ART OF STILLNESS

The next morning, Ava expected action—maybe a test of grit, a hike through the jungle, or a deep dive into martial arts. Instead, Bodhi greeted her in silence, holding a small bronze bell in his hand.

The bell itself was small but striking—a Thai-style *ghanta* crafted from bronze, with subtle etchings of lotus petals around its base and a tiny Bodhi leaf carved into the handle. It had clearly aged with dignity; its patina told stories of sun, rain, and a thousand meditations. When Bodhi held it, he did so with reverence, as though it were not merely an object but a teacher.

He rang it gently—never rushed, never forceful.

The sound that followed wasn't just a noise. It was a presence.

A long, clear tone that shimmered like morning light on water, echoing through the trees and settling deep into the bones.

"This bell," Bodhi explained, "is not just to start meditation. It calls the mind home. It reminds us to return—to the breath, to the body, to this moment. It symbolizes the purity of life and the impermanence of thought."

Each time it rang, Ava could feel herself softening—like clay in the sun, shaped by silence.

He raised it gently and gave it a single, resonant ring.

Dinggggggggg.

The sound shimmered through the humid air like a ripple across still water.

"This," Bodhi said, "marks the beginning of the day. The bell reminds us to return to the present moment. To cleanse the mind. To begin again."

He led her outside and pointed to a flat stone beneath a palm tree.

"Sit. Breathe. Let go."

Ava looked at the stone. Then at Bodhi. "For how long?"

Bodhi shrugged with a small smile. "Until the lesson is learned."

Before she could fire off a follow-up question, he turned and walked away—disappearing into the dense green like a monk-shaped whisper.

So, she sat.

At first, her thoughts were louder than the jungle.

What was this? A patience test? A prank? A tropical timeout?

She shifted, scratched, sighed, and mentally composed a dramatic monologue about how stillness was definitely not her learning style.

But then, another bell rang from the hut.

Dinggggggggggg.

This time, the sound didn't irritate her. It nudged her.

She breathed.

And she noticed—really noticed.

The way the leaves shimmered like sequins when the sun hit them just right.

The chorus of insects playing percussion in the underbrush.

The rhythm of her own breath syncing with the wind.

With each bell that echoed through the day, Ava felt her thoughts unclench.

Stillness wasn't punishment. It was permission.

And for the first time in years, she wasn't doing anything—and yet, she was fully alive.

THE STORY OF THE TIGER & THE MONK

As the sun dipped lower, Bodhi returned, carrying two small bowls of rice and vegetables.

He handed one to Ava and sat beside her, eating in silence for a few minutes before finally speaking.

"A long time ago," he began, "a young monk asked his master, 'What must I do to achieve enlightenment?'"

Ava paused mid-bite, knowing by now that every story had a lesson buried inside it.

Bodhi continued, "The master took him into the jungle and told him to sit in stillness until he found his answer. The monk sat for many days, waiting for wisdom to strike."

"One morning, a tiger appeared."

Ava's grip tightened around her bowl.

"The monk froze. The tiger stared at him, its golden eyes unblinking. Fear gripped the monk's heart. He wanted to run, but he remembered his master's words. Instead, he breathed. He accepted the moment. He became still."

Ava swallowed. "What happened?"

"The tiger sniffed the air, then walked away. It did not see him as prey. It saw him as part of the jungle. When the monk returned to his master, the master smiled and said, 'Now, you understand. You were never meant to control the jungle. You were meant to become one with it.'"

Stillness wasn't punishment.
It was permission.

Ava sat with that.

She had spent her entire career trying to control her surroundings—her team, her company, her future.

But what if true strength wasn't in control, but in stillness?

What if she had been running from her own tiger all along?

Bodhi stood. "Tomorrow, we chop wood, carry water."

Ava nodded, not questioning him this time.

She understood now.

Some lessons had to be learned through stillness before action.

CHOP WOOD, CARRY WATER

The next morning, Bodhi woke her before dawn with a ring of the ghanta.

Dinggggggggggg.

He handed her an axe and two buckets.

"Chop wood," he said.

Ava sighed. "For how long?"

He smiled. "Until you stop thinking about how long."

She groaned and got to work.

The first thirty minutes were miserable.

The first hour was exhausting.

But by the second hour, her brain went quiet.

She wasn't thinking about work, or stress, or the emails she wasn't answering.

She was just swinging the axe.

When Bodhi saw that she had finally stopped overthinking it, he nodded.

Then, he handed her the two buckets.

"Now, carry water."

Ava sighed. "Of course. Of course we need water."

The well was down the hill, and each step back up felt like a workout designed by an ancient sadist.

But when she set the full buckets down next to the wood, Bodhi smiled.

"Now, we have fire. Now, we have water."

That evening, after dinner, he finally spoke more than a few words.

"There is an old Zen proverb," he said as he poured her Ceylon tea.

"A young monk once asked his master, 'What is enlightenment?'

The master replied, 'Before enlightenment, chop wood, carry water.'

'And after enlightenment?' the monk asked.

The master smiled. 'After enlightenment, chop wood, carry water.'"

Ava frowned. "So … nothing changes?"

Bodhi shook his head. "Everything changes. Because now, you see the task for what it is. Not a burden, but a way to live."

Ava thought about all the times she had tried to avoid the small tasks—at work, in life.

She had always chased big wins.

But maybe success wasn't about the big moments.

Maybe it was about doing the small things, every day, with presence and purpose.

THE RITUAL OF THE MORNING BELL

The next morning, Ava woke up before the ghanta rang. As she chopped wood and carried water up the hill, she heard the *dingggggggggg…*

Then she sat next to Bodhi as he meditated, the morning sun casting golden light through the trees.

The ghanta rang.

Dingggggggggg.

She inhaled.

The bell rang.

Dinggggggggg.

She exhaled.

For twenty minutes, they sat in silence.

For the first time, Ava didn't fidget. She didn't check the time.

She was just there.

Afterward, Bodhi finally spoke.

"Small rituals create strong minds."

Ava thought about her mornings back in San Francisco.

Wake up. Check phone. Scroll through stress. React to problems before even getting out of bed.

Maybe the problem wasn't her schedule.

Maybe it was her lack of a ritual.

THE LAST LESSON – CARRY IT WITH YOU

The next morning, before the ghanta rang, Ava chopped wood without hesitation.

She carried water without complaint.

She rang the morning ghanta before Bodhi could.

And when he handed her a black box, she wasn't surprised.

Inside—

A tiny wooden door carving.

A handwritten note:

"You found B – Behaviors & Rituals. Go to Brazil."

And—of course—another plane ticket.

Ava looked up. "What if I forget all of this when I go home?"

Bodhi smiled. "You won't. Because now, you have rituals."

She slipped the carving in her bag, feeling the weight of everything she had learned.

She wasn't just leaving Thailand.

She was bringing it with her.

The journey goes on.

PRACTICAL EXERCISES TO DO:

1. **Chop Wood, Carry Water Challenge:** Choose one daily habit and do it with full presence (making your bed, washing dishes, brushing teeth, walking the dog). Small actions done mindfully build discipline.

2. **Digital Fasting:** Remove one digital distraction (phone notifications, emails, social media) for one full day and observe how much clarity and focus you gain.

3. **Ritual Building:** Pick one new ritual (morning meditation, journaling, exercise) and commit for 30 days.

UNCONVENTIONAL EXERCISES:

1. **The Reverse Routine Challenge:** Change one major daily habit (switch your morning/evening routine, take a different commute, eat dinner for breakfast). See how it disrupts automatic thinking and forces presence.

2. **The 3-Day Digital Purge:** Delete ALL social media, news, and non-essential apps for three days. Observe your stress, boredom, and brain space.

3. **The Power of One-Minute Rituals:** Pick three small rituals (lighting a candle before deep work, playing a song before meetings, a 60-second body stretch every hour). See how tiny rituals create big momentum.

5 PRACTICAL TOOLS FOR BEHAVIORS & RITUALS:

1. **Consistency Over Motivation:** Habits win over inspiration every time.

2. **Stack Habits:** Attach a new habit to an existing one (ex: meditate after brushing your teeth). (Note from the author: I do yoga while meditating.)

3. **Master Transitions:** Create a start-of-day and end-of-day ritual to mentally switch between work and life. (Note from the author: I do 20 minutes of stationary bike every morning and evening.)

4. **Remove Friction:** Make habits easier by reducing barriers (put your workout clothes next to your bed).

5. **Celebrate Small Wins:** Your brain releases dopamine when you celebrate tiny milestones.

NEUROSCIENCE FACTS ON HABITS & RITUALS:

- **The Basal Ganglia & Habit Formation:** Repetition strengthens neural pathways, making behaviors automatic over time.
- **Dopamine & Rituals:** Even simple rituals trigger dopamine, reinforcing consistency.
- **Cognitive Load Reduction:** Routine behaviors free mental space for deeper thinking and creativity.

CONCLUSION & TAKEAWAYS:

→ **Your rituals define your reality.**

→ **Habits create structure**; structure creates freedom.

→ **Excellence is not an act, but a habit.**

CHAPTER 4

E – ENVIRONMENT & SPACE

The Atmosphere of Success

WELCOME TO BRAZIL – THE CLUTTERED MIND

Ava stepped off the plane in Rio de Janeiro and straight into what felt like a wall of wet heat. It was the kind of thick, sticky air that wrapped around you like an unwanted hug from a sweaty stranger.

The smells hit her next—salt from the ocean, grilled meats from some unseen street vendor, and the faint scent of ripe fruit that made her stomach growl.

She pulled out the now-familiar black box from her bag and read the note inside:

"Go to Brazil. Find Luzia."

No last name. No instructions. No address.

Just vibes.

THE PICKUP: LUZIA & THE BROKEN JEEP

Before Ava could even begin to process how she was supposed to find someone with zero information, a battered yellow Jeep skidded to a stop in front of her.

The driver's door flew open and out stepped a woman straight out of a Brazilian action movie—aviator sunglasses, sun-kissed skin, hair tied up in a messy bun, and the undeniable energy of someone who had seen and done it all.

The woman pulled off her sunglasses and squinted at her. "Ava?"

Ava hesitated. "Uh … Luzia?"

Luzia grinned, grabbed Ava's bag, and threw it into the back of the Jeep, which smelled like sunscreen, coconut, and gasoline.

"Hop in."

Ava eyed the Jeep. It looked like it had lived through multiple wars.

She climbed in. "So… are you my mentor?"

Luzia revved the engine, which coughed like a dying animal before roaring to life. "That depends. Are you here to listen, or just to hear yourself talk?"

Ava opened her mouth—then thought better of it.

Luzia smirked. "Good start."

And with that, she floored the gas, sending them barreling through the streets of Rio, dodging cars, mopeds, and the occasional loose chicken.

They finally arrived at a modest beach house tucked between overgrown palms and wild bougainvillea. The home looked like it had been stitched together from the memories of other homes—scraps of wood, corrugated metal, and weathered concrete. It was quaint but full of character, with string lights zigzagging across the porch and a blue barrel tucked in the corner to collect rainwater. It wasn't luxury, but it had soul.

Luzia guided Ava through the creaky entryway, the smell of sea salt and driftwood clinging to the air. She pointed to a small room at the end of the narrow hallway. Its entrance was framed by a pair of French doors that looked like they'd lived a whole life before arriving here—weathered paint peeling at the edges, iron handles slightly rusted, and panes of glass that rippled like old water. They had clearly been salvaged from somewhere else, but someone had lovingly restored them just enough to be functional. When Ava opened them, they groaned softly, revealing a breathtaking view of the water just beyond the brush-covered dunes.

Inside, the room was simple but soulful: a narrow bed in the corner with a patchwork quilt, and a three-legged stool doubling as a nightstand, balancing slightly unevenly on the worn wooden floor. The walls were painted a soft, sandy white, and a woven reed mat covered part of the floor. It wasn't much—but it was enough. Honest, unpolished, and just right.

"Go to sleep, see you in the morning." Luzia said smiling.

THE ART OF CREATING SPACE

Ava woke up to the sound of waves crashing outside.

The small beachside house was simple but had a soul—wooden floors, big open windows, the smell of brewed coffee and something sweet wafting in from the kitchen.

Morning Rituals Begin

Luzia was already outside on the beach, stretching like a panther ready to hunt.

Ava, still half-asleep, dragged herself out of bed and joined her.

Luzia handed her a steaming cup of Brazilian coffee. "First rule of success: Take care of your space. That starts with your mind."

She motioned for Ava to sit.

"Before the world tells you what to do, decide for yourself."

Ava raised an eyebrow. "And how do I do that?"

Luzia stared. "You start here."

Ava's New Morning Rituals:

- 5:00 AM Wake-Up (ugh, but fine, just chop wood and carry water)
- 20 Minutes of Meditation (train the mind before the world distracts it)
- 20 Minutes of Yoga (because stillness and movement go together)
- Journaling (write three things that are on her mind, clear them out)
- Walk on the Beach Without Her Phone (being present, no scrolling)

Ava took a deep breath, feeling the ocean breeze on her skin.

For the first time in a long time, she wasn't starting the day reacting to notifications.

She was creating space.

THE MENTAL DECLUTTER

After breakfast, Luzia handed Ava a notebook and pen.

"Write down everything taking up space in your mind. No filter."

Ava frowned at the blank page.

Then—the floodgates opened.

- The company.
- Investor pressure.

- Leadership challenges.
- The creeping feeling that success wasn't enough.

Fifteen minutes later, her hand ached.

Luzia took the pages and, without hesitation, ripped them out and threw them into a small fire pit.

Ava gasped. "HEY!"

Luzia shrugged. "Holding onto junk won't help you? Burn it. Make space."

Ava watched the flames eat her thoughts.

For the first time in months, she felt lighter.

THE PHYSICAL DECLUTTER – LESS IS MORE

The next morning, Ava woke up to Luzia dragging furniture out of the house.

"Are you moving?" Ava asked groggily.

Luzia tossed her a cardboard box. "Nope. You are."

Ava stared at the box. "Another metaphor?"

Luzia grinned. "You're catching on."

Lessons from Luzia:

- Your environment affects your mind.
- The more stuff you have, the more distractions you carry.
- If it doesn't serve you, let it go.

Ava thought about her San Francisco apartment—cluttered desk, books she never read, clothes she never wore.

Was it helping her or just mental noise in physical form?

She had her answer.

THE JABUTICABA TREE

It was the kind of warm Brazilian night where the air was thick with the scent of damp earth and sweet, overripe fruit bursting open in the heat.

Luzia tapped the rim of her glass. "You ever hear the story of the jabuticaba tree?"

Ava pouted. "If this is another metaphor, I'm bracing myself."

Luzia grinned. "You should."

She leaned back and continued.

"When I was a little girl, my grandfather had a jabuticaba tree in our backyard. It was magical. The fruit doesn't grow on the branches like other trees—it grows straight out of the trunk, like little dark pearls."

Ava raised an eyebrow. "That sounds … kind of weird."

Luzia nodded. "It is. But it's beautiful. And it only grows when it's ready, never before. You can't rush it. You can't force it. And if you try to pick it too early, it's bitter. But if you wait—if you let nature do what it needs to do—the fruit is the sweetest thing you'll ever taste."

She picked up a stone and tossed it into the waves.

"One summer, I was impatient. I wanted the fruit before it was ready, so I climbed up and started yanking them off. My grandfather saw me, but he didn't stop me. He just waited."

Ava smirked. "I'm guessing this didn't end well?"

Luzia chuckled. "Nope. I bit into one, and it was so sour I spit it out. My grandfather just laughed and said, 'You see? Life will always give you what you want if you take it. But if you wait, it will give you what you need.'"

Life will always give you what you want if you take it. But if you wait, it will give you what you need.

Ava sat with the words for a moment.

Then, almost instinctively, she said, "Like an unripe mango."

Luzia raised an eyebrow. "Huh?"

Ava took a slow breath. "Back in Thailand, Bodhi gave me a mango, but it wasn't just about the fruit—it was about timing. He told me that an unripe mango can't be ripened in the fridge. You can try to force it to be ready, but it'll never be as good as one that ripens naturally on the tree."

Luzia smiled, tapping the table. "Exactly. You're connecting the dots now."

Ava exhaled, shaking her head. "I've spent my whole life trying to rush things. My company, my success, my next move. I've been forcing things to happen on my schedule instead of letting them develop on their own."

Luzia leaned forward. "And how's that been working for you?"

Ava laughed dryly. "Like biting into a bitter jabuticaba."

Luzia clinked her glass against Ava's. "Then stop picking fruit before it's ready."

FREEING THE MIND THROUGH DANCE

That night, Luzia dragged Ava to a samba school rehearsal.

The air pulsed with drumbeats, bodies moving in perfect sync.

Luzia leaned in. "This is focus."

Ava watched, mesmerized.

No one was distracted. Everyone was fully present. Then—Luzia pulled her onto the dance floor.

Ava panicked. "Nope. Nope, nope—"

Too late.

Luzia laughed. "Dance. Move. Get out of your head."

Ava hesitated—then, something clicked.

She let go.

She danced like she was a kid again.

She was the music.

She was the space between the beats.

She was free.

THE DAY I LET GO OF MY OLD LIFE

Luzia and Ava sat on the beach, the waves rolling in with the rhythm of a slow samba, the firelight flickering between them.

Luzia took a sip of her caipirinha before speaking. "I used to have your life."

Ava blinked. "You ran a startup?"

Luzia chuckled. "No. But I ran. And I never stopped."

She leaned back on her elbows, gazing at the stars.

"I was a lawyer in São Paulo. Big firm, long hours, fancy title, fancier car. Everything looked perfect on paper. But every morning, I woke up with this weight on my chest—like I was trapped inside a life that didn't belong to me."

Ava nodded slowly. That feeling? She knew it well.

"One day, I was in court, representing a client I didn't believe in, fighting for something I didn't care about. And suddenly, I couldn't breathe. Right there, in the middle of the trial, I just … walked out."

Ava sat up straighter. "You walked out? Just like that?"

Luzia nodded. "I left my briefcase, my notes, my entire case. I walked straight out of the building, took a cab to the airport, and bought a one-way ticket to Bahia. I had never been there. I just knew I had to go."

Ava's mouth fell open. "What did your boss say? Your clients?"

Luzia grinned. "Oh, they were furious. But you know what? The world kept spinning. And I learned that the life I had built wasn't real—it was a prison I had designed for myself."

She turned to Ava, eyes twinkling. "Sometimes, we hold on so tight to a life that doesn't fit, simply because we're afraid of the empty space that comes after."

Ava felt a lump form in her throat. Because for the first time in her life, she realized—she wasn't afraid of failing. She was afraid of stopping long enough to question if she was even going in the right direction.

Sometimes, we hold on so tight to a life that doesn't fit, simply because we're afraid of the empty space that comes after.

THE TOOLS FOR CREATING SPACE

- An iron key.
- A handwritten note—"You found E – Environment & Space. Go to South Africa. Find Zola."
- And—of course—another plane ticket.

Ava's Nighttime Rituals (New & Improved):

- Review her day & write down 3 wins.
- Repeat her 5 core values aloud.
- **Affirmations before sleep:**
  - I create space for what matters.
  - I let go of what no longer serves me.

▶ I am open to growth and change.

Ava stared at the ocean—vast, open, endless.

For the first time in a long time, she didn't just see the waves. She saw the space between them.

And that? That changed everything.

KEY TOOLS TO TAKE AWAY

1. **Declutter Your Mind:** Write down worries, then destroy the paper.

2. **Declutter Your Space:** If it doesn't serve you, let it go.

3. **Turn Off Notifications:** Your focus is more valuable than constant updates.

4. **Create Rituals for Clarity:** Morning quiet time. Evening reflection.

5. **Use Movement to Release Stress:** Dance, run, breathe—move with intention.

Ava breathed in the ocean air. She wasn't just leaving Brazil. She was bringing clarity with her. *The journey goes on.*

PRACTICAL EXERCISES TO DO:

1. **Declutter Sprint:** Pick one space (desk, office, closet) and eliminate everything unnecessary. A clean sacred space creates a clear mind.

2. **Digital Detox Hour:** Turn off all notifications for 1 hour daily and focus on deep work or relaxation.

3. **The Movement Reset:** Dance, stretch, or walk before making big decisions to physically clear mental clutter.

3.5 UNCONVENTIONAL EXERCISES:

1. The "One-Year Rule": Look at every item on your desk, home, or workspace and ask: "Have I used this in the last year?" If not, remove it. Less clutter = more clarity.

1.5 "The 2-for-1 Rule": Every time you buy one thing, you get rid of two things. This is the best way to keep a decluttered space.

2. Work in a Loud Place: Try deep work in a busy café, an airport, or a street corner. If you can focus here, you can focus anywhere.

3. The Single-Task Test: Pick one task (eating, writing, listening to a song) and do ONLY that—no multitasking. Experience how much sharper your mind becomes.

5 PRACTICAL TOOLS FOR ENVIRONMENT & SPACE:

1. Your Space Reflects Your Mind: A messy environment clutters thinking.

2. Use Music & Movement to Reset: Your body influences your brain. Move before work or problem-solving. (Note from author: great thinkers use walking as a way to clear their mind and sharpen their focus. When stuck, don't reach for the chocolate-covered almonds from the pantry, take a walk instead.)

3. Kill Notifications, Save Focus: Disable all non-essential notifications to protect deep work.

4. Create Intentional Spaces: Designate specific spaces for work, rest, and creativity. Don't bring your work or any type of screens to bed; your sleep is sacred.

5. Morning & Evening Reset Rituals: Begin and end each day with a space-clearing routine.

NEUROSCIENCE FACTS ON ENVIRONMENT & FOCUS:

- **Visual Clutter & Stress:** A messy space increases cortisol (stress hormone) and decreases focus.

- **Background Noise & Productivity:** Moderate background noise (like nature sounds or music) increases concentration.

- **The Power of a 5-Minute Reset:** A 5-minute movement break restores mental clarity faster than caffeine.

CONCLUSION & TAKEAWAYS:

→ Control your space, control your mind.

→ Focus is not about discipline—it's about eliminating distractions.

→ Create space for what truly matters.

CHAPTER 5

S — SUPPORT (OR SERVICE) & LEADERSHIP

The Foundation of Excellence

ARRIVAL IN CAPE TOWN – A NEW ENERGY

The airport was alive with movement—the rhythmic shuffle of hurried travelers, the scent of jet fuel mixed with strong espresso, and the distant hum of conversations in a dozen different languages.

Ava stepped off the plane and scanned the crowd.

And there it was—a single white sheet of paper with her name scribbled in bold black ink.

The woman holding it was impossible to miss.

She stood with effortless confidence, wearing wide-legged pants that swayed as she shifted her weight, a tank top that revealed arms sculpted by movement, and a short, natural haircut that gave her an air of quiet power.

Her rich brown skin glowed under the airport lights, and behind her over-sized sunglasses, Ava could feel a gaze that was assessing her before she even spoke.

Ava took a breath and stepped forward. "Zola?"

The woman removed her sunglasses with a smirk. "You must be Ava. Welcome to Cape Town. Let's go."

Before Ava could get a word in, Zola had already grabbed her suitcase and started walking.

THE STREETS OF CAPE TOWN – A RIDE THROUGH CHAOS

Ava barely had time to catch her breath before she was thrown into the vibrant chaos of Cape Town's streets.

Zola led her straight to a rattling Tuk-Tuk, the kind that looked like it had survived a dozen near-death experiences and was held together by duct tape, hope, and the stubbornness of its driver.

The city vibrated with life.

The smells – Roasted meats sizzling from street vendors, fresh bread from tiny bakeries, sea salt from the distant waves crashing against the shore.

The sounds – The blaring of car horns, music pulsing from open windows, the rhythmic calls of vendors selling their goods.

The sights – Vibrant murals covering the walls, bright textiles hanging from market stalls, and in the distance, Table Mountain standing like a silent guardian over the city.

Ava gripped the side of the Tuk-Tuk as they swerved through traffic, dodging pedestrians, bicycles, and one very confident goat that refused to move.

Zola, on the other hand, was completely unbothered.

"You dance?" she asked suddenly.

Ava blinked. "What?"

"Do. You. Dance?" Zola repeated, enunciating each word like Ava might be hard of hearing.

Ava hesitated. "I mean … not well."

Zola grinned. "Perfect. You'll learn."

Ava narrowed her eyes. "Learn what, exactly?"

Zola leaned back, the wind whipping past her. "Leadership."

Ava didn't have time to question it.

The Tuk-Tuk screeched to a stop outside a large, worn-down building with music spilling out from the windows.

LEADERSHIP IS A DANCE

Ava barely had time to process where she was before Zola was pulling her inside.

The studio was packed—people of all ages, all backgrounds, moving together as if they shared one heartbeat.

Ava stood frozen, watching as pairs swayed, turned, and stepped in perfect time.

Zola clapped her hands, and the music momentarily softened.

"New student!" she announced, nodding toward Ava.

Before Ava could protest, a man with a bright yellow bandanna grabbed her hand and pulled her onto the dance floor.

"Relax," he said with a grin. "Just follow my lead."

That's when Ava realized—she had no control.

She was being led.

And she hated it.

She kept anticipating the wrong steps, overthinking every movement, stiffening up instead of flowing with the rhythm.

She was used to controlling everything.

But here, control was useless.

Zola watched from the sidelines, arms crossed. "You're fighting it."

"Because I don't know what I'm doing!" Ava shot back.

Zola smiled. "Exactly. That's why you need to trust."

Her partner spun her effortlessly, and for one moment—one small, fleeting moment—she let go.

And suddenly, she was dancing.

Zola clapped. "See? Leadership is like this. You don't always have to lead from the front. Sometimes, the best thing you can do … is trust the people around you."

Ava's breath hitched.

Because that was exactly what she had been doing wrong back at her company.

She wasn't leading. She was micromanaging. She wasn't trusting. She was controlling.

The music swelled, and Ava let herself sink into the moment.

For the first time in her life … she wasn't leading.

She was learning.

ZOLA'S HOME ABOVE THE DANCE STUDIO

By the time they reached Zola's apartment above the studio, Ava was completely drained.

She expected a quiet place to unwind. She was wrong.

The music from below didn't stop. The bassline shook the floorboards; the sound of stomping feet and clapping hands echoed through the walls.

Zola, unfazed, tossed Ava a blanket.

"Couch is yours."

Ava stared at it. "Is this… a test?"

Zola grinned. "Everything is a test."

Ava collapsed onto the couch, exhausted but restless.

At first, the music was too much. But eventually, her body surrendered.

She fell asleep—not to silence, but to the rhythm of the city.

THE STRENGTH OF PERSONAL SUPPORT NETWORKS

The next morning, Ava found Zola sitting by a fire pit, staring at the ocean.

She gestured for her to sit. "You want to be a great leader, yes?"

Ava nodded.

"Then answer me this: Who holds you up?"

Ava blinked. "Uh… me?"

Zola laughed. "That's cute. And wrong." She tossed a small stick into the fire. "You ever heard the story of the lone elephant?"

Ava shook her head.

"A young elephant was separated from her herd," Zola began. "She thought, 'I'm strong. I'm independent. I don't need anyone.' So, she walked alone."

Ava crossed her arms. "Sounds efficient."

Zola raised an eyebrow. "For a while, maybe. But then, she got tired. She got lost. And she realized—without the herd, she had no protection. No guidance. No warmth. Alone, she was vulnerable. Together, they were unstoppable."

Zola turned to Ava. "So, I ask again. Who holds you up?"

Ava thought about it.

She had spent so much time trying to be the strong, independent founder.

But who had been there when she crumbled?

Who had kept her going when she wanted to quit?

She had a herd. She just never acknowledged it.

The Morning Rituals & Zola's Story

Ava's Morning Rituals (New & Improved):

- 5:00 AM Wake-Up – No alarms, no screens. Just instinct.
- 20 Minutes of Meditation – Clearing space before chaos.
- 20 Minutes of Movement – Stretching, feeling present.
- Journaling – No overthinking. Just clarity.
- Tea, Not Technology – No phone until after her rituals.

When she finished, Zola was already waiting with steaming cups of tea.

"You slept through the music," Zola said.

Ava shrugged. "I think my body gave up fighting it."

Zola nodded approvingly. "Good. That means you're starting to let go."

She took a sip of tea and leaned back.

"You know, I used to think leadership was about proving myself. About showing people I was strong. But I learned the hard way—it's not about being strong. It's about making others strong."

Ava's curiosity piqued. "How did you learn that?"

Zola's lips curled into a knowing smile. "It started when I was fifteen."

She set down her cup.

"I thought leadership was about control. Until I lost it completely."

And with that, she began her story.

ZOLA'S STORY: THE FIRST LESSON IN LEADERSHIP

"I grew up in a small village outside of Cape Town. Life wasn't easy, but we made the best of it. I had six younger siblings—six. And as the eldest, that meant one thing: I was responsible."

Ava chuckled. "The original leadership training program—older sibling survival school."

Zola laughed. "Exactly. No days off. No performance reviews. No paycheck."

She took another sip of tea, then continued.

"One day, my mother fell sick. I mean, really sick. She could barely get out of bed. My father was working far away, so suddenly, I was in charge. Not just of my siblings—but of everything. Cooking, cleaning, getting everyone ready for school, making sure the house didn't fall apart. And I thought— okay, I can handle this. I'll be tough. I'll take control."

Ava nodded. "And did it work?"

Zola simpered. "Not even a little."

She set down her cup.

"For the first few days, I tried to do everything myself. I micromanaged every little thing—how my brothers tied their shoes, how my sisters folded the laundry. And you know what happened?"

Ava shook her head.

"They rebelled." Zola laughed. "I mean full-blown mutiny. One day, I walked into the kitchen, and my youngest brother—four years old—was standing on a chair, stirring a pot of boiling water with a stick. My sisters had completely given up on cleaning. And my twelve-year-old brother just looked at me and said, 'Zola, you are the worst boss ever.'"

Ava burst out laughing.

Zola grinned. "And that's when it hit me. I wasn't leading. I was just con-trolling. I was so busy trying to do everything right that I never gave them the chance to step up. And they WANTED to help. They just didn't want to be treated like they were useless."

She leaned in, voice softer now.

"So, I changed. I started teaching them instead of ordering them. I let them make mistakes, and instead of fixing everything, I helped them figure it out themselves. And you know what happened?"

Ava raised an eyebrow. "They stopped rebelling?"

Zola nodded. "Not only that—they took ownership. My little brother started setting the table every night without being asked. My sisters divided up the chores themselves. Even my twelve-year-old brother—the one who called me 'the worst boss ever'—started helping my mother without complaining." She smiled. "And that's when I understood leadership. It's not about doing everything alone. It's about making sure no one feels alone."

AVA'S REALIZATION

Ava sat back, letting the words settle.

For years, she had been trying to do everything herself—shouldering every decision, carrying every failure, micromanaging people because she was terrified of losing control.

And what had it led to? People quitting. Resentment. A company culture that felt more like survival mode than teamwork.

She had been running a company. But she hadn't been leading it.

Zola watched her, as if reading her thoughts. "So, tell me, Ava," she said, finishing her tea. "Are you trying to prove you're strong? Or are you trying to make others strong?"

Ava didn't answer right away. She just stared into her cup of tea, watching the ripples on the surface.

For the first time, she wasn't sure which answer scared her more.

Zola handed Ava a notebook and a pen. "Write down the names of the people who support you. Personally. Professionally."

Ava hesitated, then started writing.

- Her best friend, who always reminded her that she was more than her career.
- Her co-founder, Morgan, who had stuck with her through every crisis.

- Her parents, who never fully understood her work but supported her anyway.
- Her team, who still believed in her, even when she doubted herself.

She looked at the list. It was longer than she expected.

"Good leaders don't stand alone," Zola said, reading over her shoulder. "They stand on the shoulders of others. Recognizing that doesn't make you weak. It makes you powerful."

Ava nodded, taking it in.

BUILDING TRUST & PSYCHOLOGICAL SAFETY – THE LEAP OF FAITH

The next afternoon, Zola dragged Ava back to the dance studio, much to her protest.

"Why are we doing this again?" she groaned. "I already learned to let go and follow your lead."

Zola smirked. "You learned to follow. Now, you need to learn to trust."

Ava narrowed her eyes. "Aren't those the same thing?"

Zola shook his head. "Nope. Trust is different. Following is passive. Trust is active. Trust is knowing someone has your back even when you can't see them."

Ava crossed her arms. "And how exactly are we going to learn that?"

Zola grinned mischievously. "We're going to do a blind jump."

Ava's stomach dropped. "A WHAT?"

Zola pointed to the center of the dance floor, where a couple was demonstrating the move.

The woman closed her eyes, turned her back, and jumped backwards into her partner's arms—completely blind.

No hesitation. No doubt. Just pure trust.

And the partner? Caught her effortlessly.

Ava felt her throat tighten.

Absolutely not.

THE STORY OF THE ACROBAT & THE NET

Zola must have seen the terror on Ava's face, because she pulled her aside. "You ever heard the story of the acrobat and the net?"

Ava shook her head, still eyeing the dancers like they were about to commit an actual crime against physics.

Zola leaned against the mirrored wall. "There was once an acrobat who wanted to walk the tightrope over a deep canyon. But every time he tried, he hesitated. He thought about the fall. He thought about the danger. And so, he never took the first step."

Ava nodded. "Seems reasonable."

Zola grinned. "But one day, an old man came to him and said, 'I will build you a net. That way, if you fall, you'll be caught.'"

Ava raised an eyebrow. "Smart man."

Zola tilted her head. "Maybe. But do you know what happened next?"

Ava shrugged.

Zola smiled. "The acrobat still didn't cross the rope."

Ava blinked. "Wait—why?"

"Because the problem was never the fall. The problem was his lack of trust in himself."

Ava exhaled slowly.

"The net was always there," Zola continued. "Just like your team is there. Just like the people in your life are there. But trust isn't just about knowing you'll be caught—it's about believing you deserve to be caught."

Ava felt something shift inside her.

She thought about all the times she had tried to do things alone.

All the times she had been afraid to let go because she didn't fully believe anyone would be there.

Zola patted her shoulder. "So, are you gonna jump?"

Ava took a deep breath.

And stepped onto the dance floor.

THE LEAP OF FAITH

She stood with her back to Zola, heart hammering in her chest.

"Close your eyes," she instructed.

Ava gulped but did as she was told.

"Now, jump back."

Her body screamed at her not to.

This went against every instinct she had.

And yet—

She took a breath—

And jumped.

For a split second, she was freefalling.

Then—Zola caught her, steady and unshaken.

Ava's entire body relaxed.

She did it.

And she was caught.

Zola set her down gently and grinned. "See? You had a net all along."

Ava laughed breathlessly.

And for the first time in a long time, she actually felt safe.

THE TRUST FACTOR: HOW TO CREATE PSYCHOLOGICAL SAFETY IN ANY TEAM

Later that evening as they sat by the beach, Zola explained.

"That wasn't just about the jump, Ava. That was about what great leaders do." Zola gestured to the ocean. "A leader creates a space where people feel safe enough to take risks, to fail, and to grow. That's psychological safety."

Ava thought about her own company.

A leader creates a space where people feel safe enough to take risks, to fail, and to grow.

How many people held back their ideas?

How many feared making mistakes?

How many didn't feel safe enough to jump?

"Great leaders don't just demand trust," Zola said. "They create environments where trust can exist."

Ava nodded, the lesson hitting deep.

THE FINAL BLACK BOX

On her last day, Zola handed Ava one final black box.

She had expected another exotic destination. Another faraway land. Another cryptic note telling her to seek, explore, learn.

But this time, when she opened the black box, it was different.

Inside was a plane ticket home.

Tucked underneath it, a handwritten note:

"Go home. You're ready to change your world."

Ava swallowed hard.

For weeks, she had been wandering—from the burning sands of the Moroccan desert to the quiet teahouses of Kyoto, from the humid jungles of Thailand to the electric pulse of Rio, to the powerful landscapes of South Africa. She had let go, broken down, rebuilt.

And now … it was time to go back and apply it all.

The journey goes on… at home.

5 TOOLS FOR BUILDING SUPPORT & LEADERSHIP

1. **The Leap of Faith Test:** Trust isn't built through words. It's built through action. Find ways to create moments where you and your team prove to each other that trust exists.

2. **Psychological Safety First:** Make sure people feel safe to speak up, make mistakes, and take risks. Without this, innovation dies.

3. **Know Your Net:** Identify who supports you, both professionally and personally. Trust isn't about control—it's about knowing who has your back.

4. **Lead by Letting Go:** Micromanagement is the enemy of trust. Empower people, let them take ownership, and they'll rise to the challenge.

5. **Give More Than You Take:** The best leaders don't just receive support—they give it back. Mentor, uplift, and create more leaders, not followers.

PRACTICAL EXERCISES TO DO:

1. **The Blind Guide Exercise:** Pair up with someone and take turns being blindfolded. The other person's job is to guide you through an obstacle course (this can be a simple office or outdoor path). The guide

can only give verbal instructions—no touching or physically leading. Afterward, reflect on the experience. How did it feel to depend entirely on someone else's guidance? Did you trust their instructions? This exercise strengthens communication and trust under uncertainty.

2. **The Leadership Mirror:** Ask three people you trust (friend, co-worker, mentor) to give honest feedback on how you show up as a leader. Are you supportive? Do you create space for others? Do you listen more than you talk?

3. **The Ownership Audit:** Make a list of three to five recent challenges or mistakes in your work or personal life. Then, categorize them into:

   • What I controlled

   • What was out of my control

   • How I responded

   Look at the patterns—are you taking full ownership of what you can change? Are you blaming external factors too often? Trust in leadership grows when people take responsibility rather than deflect blame.

4. **The Support Map:** Draw a map of your personal and professional support system. Identify who uplifts you, who challenges you, and where you lack support. Build stronger relationships where needed.

UNCONVENTIONAL EXERCISES:

1. **The 30-Day Give Challenge:** Give without expecting anything back—advice, mentorship, a small act of service every day for 30 days. Observe how leadership is about contribution, not power.

2. **The "No-Title" Test:** Introduce yourself without mentioning your job title for an entire week. Notice how it shifts the way people interact with you.

3. **The "Five People" Author:** Jim Rohn said, "You are the average of the five people you spend the most time with." Write down your five. Are they pushing you forward or pulling you back?

5 PRACTICAL TOOLS FOR SUPPORT & LEADERSHIP:

1. **Build Trust with Small Wins:** Trust isn't built with grand gestures—it's built with consistent, reliable actions over time.

2. **Create Psychological Safety:** Make it safe for your team to speak up, take risks, and make mistakes. The best ideas come from people who aren't afraid to fail.

3. **Lead by Listening, Not Commanding:** Great leaders don't just give orders—they ask questions, listen deeply, and empower others.

4. **Find & Nurture Your Mentors:** No one succeeds alone. Actively seek out people who have walked the path before you and learn from them.

5. **Give More Than You Take:** The best leaders aren't just supported—they support others. Pay it forward and create a culture of mentorship.

NEUROSCIENCE FACTS ON SUPPORT & LEADERSHIP:

- **Oxytocin & Trust:** When we feel supported, our brain releases oxytocin (the "trust hormone"), deepening bonds and fostering collaboration.

- **The Power of Mirror Neurons:** Leaders who display calm, confident, and compassionate behavior activate mirror neurons in their team, creating a ripple effect of positive leadership.

- **Dopamine & Psychological Safety:** Environments where people feel safe to take risks increase dopamine, leading to higher creativity, engagement, and problem-solving.

- **Neural Networks & Leadership Growth:** The more you practice mentorship and leadership skills, the stronger the neural pathways become, making leadership a natural part of your behavior.

CONCLUSION & TAKEAWAYS:

→ Great leadership isn't about power—it's about **influence and trust**.

→ Support is a **two-way street**—find your mentors and be a mentor.

→ A strong team isn't built on fear—it's built on **psychological safety**.

→ **Giving back** strengthens the culture you want to see.

→ **Trust is the foundation of leadership**. Without it, nothing works.

CHAPTER 6

THE GREAT CULTURE RESET

THE FLIGHT HOME

Ava had a window seat. A small victory.

The cabin, however, smelled like a mix of rancid barf, sweaty socks, and cheap cologne.

For the first time in her life, it didn't bother her.

She leaned her forehead against the cool glass, watching the city lights below shrink into tiny specks.

She pulled out her notebook, the one she had carried across the world, and turned to a fresh page.

And she wrote.

V – VALUES & BELIEFS (ABDI, MOROCCO)

Item from the Box: A brass compass

"The desert stripped me down to nothing,
but that's where I found everything."

Abdi—the desert traveler, the guide, the survivor—taught me what it meant to navigate life by my own values, not the expectations of others.

He handed me a compass, but it wasn't for the desert—it was for my life.

In the sand, under the stars, I faced the truth: I had lost my direction. I had spent years chasing validation, success, achievement, thinking they would fulfill me. But without values to anchor me, I was just drifting.

I learned that our values are our true north. And when we ignore them, we get lost—not in the desert, but in our own lives.

I – INTERACTIONS & COMMUNICATION (KENJI, JAPAN)

Item from the Box: A delicate ceramic teacup

"Silence speaks louder than words, if you listen."

Kenji, in the quiet of a Kyoto teahouse, handed me a teacup—fragile, yet strong. He taught me something I had never truly understood: Listening is an art.

For years, I had been hearing but not listening. I interrupted. I planned my responses instead of absorbing. I filled silences because they made me uncomfortable.

But in Japan, I sat in stillness. I learned that the best leaders don't command the room with their voice; they command it with their presence.

I held that teacup in my hands, realizing that communication is like pouring tea—you must be careful, intentional, and aware of when to stop.

Now, I understand. Real connection isn't about speaking more—it's about listening better.

B – BEHAVIORS & RITUALS (BODHI, THAILAND)

Item from the Box: A smooth river stone

"Chop wood, carry water, and repeat."

Bodhi showed me that transformation doesn't happen in the grand moments—it happens in small, daily rituals.

Before Thailand, my habits were a mess. I lived on autopilot, reacting instead of creating.

But Bodhi made me wake up at 5 a.m. He made me meditate. Move. Reflect. Not because morning routines are trendy, but because they shape who we become.

He handed me a river stone, smooth from years of being shaped by water. "Discipline is like this stone," he told me. "It starts rough, but over time, it becomes something refined."

A disciplined mind creates a disciplined life. And a disciplined life isn't restrictive—it's freeing.

A disciplined life isn't restrictive—it's freeing.

E – ENVIRONMENT & SPACE (LUZIA, BRAZIL)

Item from the Box: A tiny wooden door carving

> *"If you want to make room for something*
> *new, you have to let go of the old."*

Luzia tore apart her house, threw things into a fire, and made me do the same.

She showed me that our external world is a reflection of our internal world. The clutter in my home, my workspace, my mind—it was all the same thing.

She made me dance, forced me to feel free in my body. She made me see that I had been holding onto things—people, habits, distractions—that were taking up space meant for something better.

Inside my final black box, she left me a tiny wooden carving of a door.

She told me, "Space isn't empty. Space is where new things can begin."

> **NOTE FROM AUTHOR:** *Sometimes unlearning old not-so-good habits is harder than learning new things. It's best to replace, not erase. Replace your old habits with new ones.*

S – SUPPORT (OR SERVICE) & LEADERSHIP (ZOLA, SOUTH AFRICA)

Item from the Box: A small iron key

> *"A leader doesn't stand above others. A leader lifts others up."*

Zola—fierce, wise, and more powerful in her presence than anyone I had ever met—showed me that leadership isn't about power or authority. It's about service and trust.

She handed me a small iron key, heavy in my palm. "Leaders don't hold power," she told me. "They hold the keys to unlock potential in others."

I had been leading wrong.

I had been trying to prove myself instead of supporting others.

But leadership isn't about being the smartest person in the room. It's about empowering others to be great.

That's the leader I want to be.

THE NAMES MATCHED THEIR PURPOSE

As Ava closed her notebook, she smiled.

For the first time, she realized how perfectly their names fit their roles.

- **Abdi (Morocco):** Servant, guide—the one who helped me find my values.
- **Kenji (Japan):** Intelligent son—who taught me to listen.
- **Bodhi (Thailand):** Awakening, enlightenment—who showed me the power of rituals and healthy habits.
- **Luzia (Brazil):** Light, illumination—who helped me clear space for what matters.
- **Zola (South Africa):** Tranquility, wisdom—who taught me that true leaders create safety.

They weren't just mentors.

They were lessons wrapped in human form.

And now, it was her turn.

Ava tucked her notebook away, leaned back in her seat, and smiled as the plane descended toward San Francisco.

She had left as one person.

She was coming home as someone entirely new.

HOME AGAIN

Ava stood at the threshold of her apartment, key in hand, backpack slung on her shoulder, and the unmistakable scent of airport coffee still lingering on her jacket. She turned the key slowly, bracing herself for what might be waiting inside: either a warm welcome or a well-deserved verbal slap.

"About time, bitch," Camila said, standing in the kitchen, arms crossed but eyes wide with relief. She wore Ava's old hoodie and no pants, which meant she'd either just woken up or emotionally refused to deal with time while Ava was gone.

Camila had been her ride-or-die since college. They had moved in together right after Stanford, realizing that their Type-A tendencies and mutual love for productivity hacks made them the perfect roommates.

Ava dropped her bags and rushed to her, wrapping her in the kind of hug that said, "I missed you and I'm sorry," all at once.

Camila held on for a moment longer than expected. "You smell like dirt, airplane nuts, and ... confidence?"

"It's BO," Ava said, grinning. "The spiritual kind."

Camila pulled back and squinted at her. "You're ... different."

Ava nodded, dropping her bags again. "Yeah. I think I finally met myself."

The two of them sat on the balcony that night, overlooking the quiet shimmer of the San Francisco Bay. A breeze moved between them like a friendly ghost. The city lights sparkled like pixels, but Ava wasn't looking at the view. She was staring at the sky, her mind still tracing constellations she'd studied in the Andes.

They talked for hours—about the desert, the silent monastery, the impossible decision to unplug, and the insane clarity that followed. Ava laughed when she realized she hadn't touched her phone for many days and didn't miss it one bit. Camila listened, skeptical at first, then finally leaned back, hand over her heart.

"Damn," Camila said. "You really went Eat, Pray, Corporate Strategy."

"I know," Ava replied, sipping mint tea. "I went out there to escape, but what I found was ... clarity."

Later that night, Camila retired to her room with a dramatic yawn and a half-hearted, "Namaste, bitch." Ava smiled and made her way into her own room.

She sat on her bed, still wearing her travel-worn jeans, and opened her notebook—the one she'd scribbled in from gate to gate, altitude to altitude. There were pages of quotes, diagrams, names, arrows, and tear-stained epiphanies.

And there it was, circled three times: "Culture starts at the root. Values. And values must be lived, not laminated."

She read through her notes slowly, the jetlag numbing her limbs but sharpening her focus. She wasn't just re-entering her old world. That world was gone. What she was doing now was stepping into a new one. The same job, same city, same coffee mug—but with a new lens.

She was about to reset everything. She knew this much:

- She would lead with values, not vague intentions.
- She would stop tolerating toxic alignment and call it what it was.

- She would lead her team, not rescue them.
- She would cultivate—not control—the culture.

Culture starts at the root. Values.

Her flight home wasn't the end of her journey. It was the beginning of her revolution.

As the city hummed in the background, Ava looked out her bedroom window and whispered the same line she had written at the top of her notes:

"Culture isn't something you fix. It's something you grow."

Tomorrow, she would replant the roots.

> **NOTE FROM AUTHOR:** *Ava went through a massive transformation and now realizes that she needs to transform the culture surrounding her at home and at work. Experiencing instead of reading or watching a "how-to" video online has a lasting impression. It's important "to do" which will translate to "to be." Transformation is as impactful as the actions. The more deliberate the action, the stickier it becomes.*

THE JOURNEY NEVER ENDS

Ava's journey wasn't just about finding herself—it was about becoming the kind of leader who elevates others.

Now, it's your turn.

Apply these lessons. Live them. Teach them.

Because true leadership isn't about what you achieve—it's about what you help others achieve.

And that?

That is how you leave a legacy.

> **NOTE FROM AUTHOR:** *Unlike Ava who is a CEO, we are not all CEOs of our own company, but we are the CEO of our lives. It doesn't matter if you have a leadership position or not, YOU need to lead your life.*

CHAPTER 7

VIBES IN ACTION

Reinventing Leadership at Home and Work

MONDAY: THE FIRST DAY BACK – CHOPPING WOOD, CARRYING WATER

Ava naturally woke up at 5:00 a.m.

She had never been a morning person, but something in her had changed. Discipline wasn't about motivation—it was about ritual.

She rolled out of bed and went straight into her new morning practice:

Ava rang her ghanta which she purchased from a little shop in China Town. That started her days going forward.

- **20 minutes of meditation:** breathing, centering, making space for clarity.
- **20 minutes of yoga:** grounding herself in her body before entering the battlefield of leadership.
- **Japanese tea ritual:** slowly pouring and drinking tea to set her intentions for the day.
- **Walking to work for 20 minutes:** no notifications, no distractions, just presence.

These are her new rings to close every morning before going to the office.

By the time she reached the office, she felt unshakable.

Her team, however? They looked shaken.

The standing meeting began. Everyone was watching her, waiting.

Ava cleared her throat.

"My grandpa used to say that traveling to new places is the best way to find clarity. I had to leave to figure out what's next for our company—and for myself. I'm back now. Things will be different. Starting right now."

She paused and let the silence cover the room. Everyone but Ava felt uncomfortable and looked around the room, eyes locking on their leader.

"Tonight, I want you to reflect on your five core values. Write them down, and we'll share them tomorrow. If we don't know what we stand for, we're just chasing money and hoping for the best. That's not leadership."

She gave another long pause.

"I also owe you time. I'll be meeting with each of you one-on-one. And I'm going to start by listening, so please speak up, this is your chance to voice your thoughts."

A few raised eyebrows. A couple of side-glances.

But no one spoke.

Good. That meant they were thinking.

THE ONE-ON-ONES – REDEFINING LEADERSHIP

Ava had spent years believing leadership was about having answers.

But leadership wasn't about being the smartest in the room.

It was about being the clearest.

And the best way to get clarity? Ask the right questions.

John, the CFO – A Matter of Trust

Ava didn't try to convince John to stay. She simply listened.

And for the first time, she truly heard him.

He wasn't leaving because he hated the job.

He was leaving because he felt unheard.

"We were running out of funds. I told you; I told the team. No one listened."

Ava nodded. "I hear you now. We have five investors who want in. But I need 100% of your focus. If you stay, I need you all in. If you leave, I'll respect that."

John's expression softened. This was different.

He took a deep breath. "Let me think about it."

That was a win.

Josh, the CRO – The Quiet Quitter

Ava studied Josh as he squirmed in his chair.

"Why are you quitting?"

Josh shrugged. "I'm not going to hit my numbers. Sales leaders leave when that happens. That's just the way it is."

Ava let silence do the heavy lifting.

One full minute.

Josh shifted. "Look, the market sucks."

Ava kept staring.

Finally, Josh sighed. "I have another job lined up."

There it was. The truth.

Ava nodded. "Then you should leave today."

Josh looked surprised. "Today?"

"You were gone three quarters ago, Josh. If you're not all in, I don't want you here."

No anger. No begging.

Just clarity.

Josh shook her hand and left.

Ava felt lighter already.

Megan, the Rising Star – The New CRO

Ava called in the only sales manager who was making her numbers, Megan.

Megan was sharp. Hungry. A Midwest hustler who treated customers like real partners.

Ava sat across from her. "Are you ready to serve the Sales team and become CRO?"

Megan's eyes didn't flicker. "Yes."

Ava smiled. "Good. You're promoted. Come back with your strategy, organizational plan, and we'll make it official tomorrow."

No ceremony. No "Are you sure?"

Just trust.

Megan nodded. She was ready.

Catherine, the CMO – The Culture Killer

Catherine walked in with her usual air of self-importance.

As soon as she sat down… "Josh was useless," she scoffed. "Good riddance. What a bad hire and waste of time. We need to rebrand, but it's going to cost. I am going to need 5x our budget to make it happen."

Ava watched her for a long moment.

Then, calmly, she said, "Catherine, you're fired."

Catherine blinked. "What?"

Ava leaned forward. "You lead with fear. Fear kills creativity, trust, and teams. You've choked the life out of marketing, and I won't allow that in our company. Pack up. You're done."

Catherine stormed out.

And just like that, the tension broke.

Fear kills creativity, trust, and teams.

Jenny, the Customer Success Officer – Finding Her Voice

Jenny was brilliant but quiet.

Too quiet.

"What happened to the major customer who left?" Ava asked.

Jenny immediately blamed the product.

Ava shook her head. "That's not what I asked."

Jenny hesitated. "I told Morgan the product needed changes, but he wouldn't listen. And eventually when Product doesn't listen, you give up."

Ava nodded. "Morgan doesn't listen unless you make him. Your team loves you, Jenny, but respect is different. Step up. Make your voice heard. I'll back you."

Jenny sat up straighter.

For the first time, she believed she had a voice.

Morgan, the CTO – The Lone Genius

Morgan loved coding more than humans. He was probably on the spectrum, which made social interactions tough.

But Ava understood him. Her sister was the same.

"You hate leading people," Ava said.

Morgan shrugged. "They don't listen. Customers are dumb."

Ava smiled. "You're a genius, but you're not a leader. You'll still be our technical visionary, but no more direct reports for you."

Morgan exhaled in relief. "Finally."

One problem solved.

But who was going to lead the Product team was another problem to solve.

Grace, the Chief of Staff – The Right Hand

Ava met Grace's eyes. "VIBES changed my life. Help me change this company."

Grace smiled. "Always."

Then, before she left, she looked at Ava's five symbolic items from her trip, neatly set on her desk.

"Interesting," she said.

Ava laughed.

They had work to do.

"I GOT YOU" – CREATING A CIRCLE OF SAFETY

Ava had spent years thinking leadership was about being the smartest in the room.

She thought it was about being the one who had all the answers, the one who carried the weight, the one who could handle everything.

But that wasn't leadership.

She had learned this lesson the hard way—falling off camels in the Moroccan desert, getting lost in the Thai jungle, burning through countless pots of tea in Kyoto. And let's not forget the samba-induced existential crisis in Brazil.

What she learned, above all, was this:

The best leaders don't stand alone. They create a circle of safety, where people can speak up, step up, and grow.

Tuesday wasn't about making decisions.

It was about creating space for the right ones to happen.

REBUILDING TRUST, ONE TEAM AT A TIME

Ava knew she had to start with Marketing.

With Catherine gone, the team looked like a bunch of released hostages— relieved but disoriented. They had spent so long operating under fear that they didn't know what to do with their sudden freedom.

Ava sat with them one by one.

She didn't start by barking orders or dictating a new strategy.

She simply asked, "What do you need?"

At first, they hesitated, looking at each other like kids unsure if they were being tricked.

Then—slowly—they started talking.

Less fear. More creativity.

Fewer pointless meetings. More collaboration.

Permission to try new things—without being ripped apart if they failed.

Ava listened.

Then she asked, "Who do you want leading this team?"

And to her surprise, they didn't have a name. Not a single one.

The previous CMO was controlling and micromanaged everything and everyone. She created an environment where people never knew when the next shoe was going to drop. As a result, the people in Marketing operated as a bunch of individuals and not a real team.

That's when Ava realized Marketing needed an entirely new leader. A new hire?

Unlike Engineering, which had a clear standout.

"WHERE THE F* WERE YOU?"**

Ava was sipping her tea when the door slammed open.

There stood Jane.

She had the kind of energy that filled a room before she even spoke. Her dark, wavy hair was tied into a loose ponytail, but it was the kind of ponytail that somehow still looked effortlessly cool, not the exhausted "I gave up today" kind.

Her frame was athletic—built from years of competitive tennis at college—broad shoulders, toned arms, like she could lift a server rack and not break a sweat.

And her presence? Sharp. Direct. No nonsense.

"Where the f*** were you?" she demanded. Her voice was low but powerful, controlled but urgent—like a coach ready to rip into a team that was blowing a championship game.

Ava smiled at her old classmate from Stanford.

She stood up, walked around the desk, and pulled Jane into a tight hug. "Jane, I love you. It's so good to see you."

Jane stiffened—then relaxed.

For all her hard-edged sarcasm and no-BS attitude, she melted in Ava's arms like a Labrador puppy.

They sat on the couch.

"I went on a spiritual journey," Ava said, grinning. "I didn't abandon ship. I just … learned a few things."

Jane raised an eyebrow. "Like what?"

Ava replied, "Like how to eat desert beetles. How to dance. How to chop wood and carry water. And how to let go of control without letting go of leadership."

Jane narrowed her eyes. "You sound … different."

Ava shrugged. "I am. But I'm still me. Just upgraded."

Jane studied her for a long moment.

Then she nodded.

"Well," she said, "since you went off on some *Eat Pray Love* quest, the Engineering team has been in absolute chaos. Morgan was already bad at managing people, and now that he's out, they're basically feral. What are we gonna do?"

Ava stayed silent.

She waited.

She watched.

And just like she had hoped—Jane stepped up.

"I'll run Engineering," Jane said, crossing her arms. "You run Product."

Ava smiled. "Done. But if you're going to be the new CTO, you need to learn how to chop wood and carry water."

Jane frowned. "What?"

Ava patted her on the shoulder. "Welcome to leadership. We start tomorrow. See you at the standing meeting."

CREATING A CULTURE OF EXTREME OWNERSHIP

With Marketing stabilizing and Jane stepping in as CTO, Ava turned to the next fires to put out.

Megan's First Sales Meeting: Ava sat in the back and just watched. Megan was ready. She was steady, confident, and she knew how to inspire people. The team followed her lead. It was the opposite of Josh's energy-sucking meetings. Ava could feel it—they were moving in the right direction.

Jenny's Customer Success Team: Ava showed up not to interfere, but to back Jenny up. She made it clear—Customer Success would not be ignored anymore. She expected them to be louder, pushier, and relentless about advocating and representing their customers' voices. Morgan was out of excuses with regards to the product's ease of use. He prioritized building instead of adapting to customer needs.

Funding Talks with John, the CFO: Ava and John had an honest conversation. She told him she wasn't interested in investors who just wanted a quick exit (i.e. IPO or selling the company for fast returns). She wanted people who believed in sustainable growth, product excellence, and company culture. John respected that she was playing the long game—and he stayed.

A Walk-and-Talk with Morgan: Ava knew Morgan would open up better if he didn't have to make eye contact. So, she took him for a walk. He was relieved to step out of leadership but still deeply invested in his product. Without mentioning Jane, Morgan volunteered her as the CTO to run Engineering. They agreed—to balance out the team, they needed a true Product leader to bridge the gap. Someone who wasn't just brilliant but could actually work with people. Jane was also a brainiac and could mind-wrestle with the best. Ava's background was all in Product, so she will take over that team until they identify the right leader.

Open Office Hours for the Remote Team: Ava blocked out two hours just for drop-ins from remote employees. She needed to rebuild trust, and that started by making herself available.

A New Company Rule: No more meetings for the sake of meetings. If a meeting could be a Slack message, it should be a Slack message.

By the end of the day, things felt different.

THE CULTURE SHIFT BEGINS

On Wednesday, Ava stood in front of the leadership team.

She picked up a marker and wrote on the whiteboard:

Integrity. Curiosity. Connection. Courage. Joy.

Then, she turned to them.

"These are my core values. What are yours?"

One by one, her team got up and wrote theirs.

Some words were different, but the overlap was striking.

And that's when it hit her.

This wasn't about rules. This wasn't about policies. This was about identity.

"We're not here to be another tech company. We're here to build something that lasts. And that starts with us."

She capped the marker.

"We align on values today. Tomorrow, we build a culture around them."

She looked at her team—the people who had survived the chaos, stuck through the storm, and were still standing.

This was it.

This was the company she was meant to lead.

And for the first time... she wasn't just hoping for a better culture.

She was creating it.

NOTE TO EMPLOYEES

In the course of the week, Ava had touched base with many employees either in person or digitally. She could feel the energy changing and a new culture shaping. She needed to send out an email to make sure everyone got the same message.

Her note:

SUBJECT: A NEW CHAPTER – OUR CULTURE, OUR FUTURE

Hi Everyone,

First of all—let's clear up some rumors.

We are **NOT** selling the company.

We are **NOT** shutting down.

We are **NOT** running out of money.

We are **NOT** doing layoffs.

But we **ARE** about to do something bold.

Over the past month, I stepped away from the noise to gain clarity. I didn't just take a trip—I took a journey. One that challenged everything I thought I knew about leadership, success, and purpose.

I learned that values are our compass—without them, we are just wandering in the desert. I learned the power of listening and precision—because the best ideas are often found in silence. I learned that greatness isn't about speed, but about discipline and consistency—chop wood, carry water. I learned that our environment shapes us, and if we want to perform at our best, we need to create space for clarity. I learned that leadership isn't about standing alone—it's about lifting others up and creating a circle of safety.

I came back a different leader.

And now, we are going to become a different company.

Starting next week, we begin our transformation.

For five days, we will focus on a different theme each day—a core element that will shape us into the company we are meant to be. This will

136

not be another corporate initiative filled with empty words. It will be an actionable shift in how we work, how we lead, and how we serve.

Our New Company Values

- **Integrity:** We do what's right, even when no one is watching.
- **Curiosity:** We seek to understand before being understood.
- **Connection:** We build relationships, not transactions.
- **Courage:** We take bold action, even when it's uncomfortable.
- **Joy:** We find meaning and fulfillment in our work.

These values will guide every decision we make. Our values put us on common ground with common vocabulary and language.

Leadership Changes & Next Steps

Megan has been promoted to **Chief Revenue Officer (CRO)**. She will lead our Sales & Customer Partnerships with a relentless focus on value.

Jane has stepped up as **Chief Technology Officer (CTO)**. As a fierce problem-solver and innovator, she will lead our Engineering team into the future.

We are actively hiring a **Chief Marketing Officer (CMO)** who embodies our values and will help us tell our story with authenticity.

I will be directly leading the **Product team** until we identify the right leader who can build products that are both powerful and user-friendly.

John, our CFO, is staying. And together, we will be raising capital from investors who believe in sustainable, people-first growth—not just an exit strategy.

What This Means for You

We are no longer just a tech company. We are a value-driven company.

We will build products that serve people—not just markets. We will create a workplace where you feel safe to speak up, take risks, and grow. We will stop doing things just because "that's the way it's always been done."

The Next 5 Days: A Culture Reset

Starting next Monday, we will focus on one theme per day:

- **Monday – V:** *Values & Beliefs* – We will align on our company values and what they mean in action.
- **Tuesday – I:** *Interactions & Communication* – We will redefine how we collaborate, listen, and create transparency.
- **Wednesday – B:** *Behaviors & Rituals* – We will embed daily habits that build long-term excellence.
- **Thursday – E:** *Environment & Space* – We will create a workspace (physically & mentally) that enhances focus and creativity.
- **Friday – S:** *Support & Leadership* – We will step up for each other, build trust, and lead with purpose.

This will be collaborative, challenging, and energizing. And we are ALL in this together.

I can't wait to build this with you. Let's make this the company we are all proud to be a part of.

See you Monday.

– Ava

AVA WRITES HER COMPANY CULTURE STATEMENT

That night, after her email went out, Ava sat alone at her kitchen table with nothing but her notebook, a lukewarm cup of tea, and a stack of sticky notes with phrases from her leadership *team. Words like trust, innovation, grit, growth, human-first*, and *integrity* floated around like sparks waiting to catch.

She thought about everything—the people who stayed, the ones who left, the walk-and-talks, the Friday wins, the hard conversations, and the culture cleanups. She knew that her job wasn't just to grow the company—but to grow the conditions where people could grow themselves.

She reviewed feedback from her executive leadership team. Grace said, "We've become a company where people can actually breathe." Jenny shared, "For the first time, I feel like I can be myself at work and still win." Megan added, "It's simple—we care, and we deliver." Even Morgan said, "We stopped trying to be perfect and started getting real."

Ava knew it was time to put this into words—not a generic mission statement or a laminated cliché, but a living, breathing declaration of what they stood for and where they were going.

OUR COMPANY CULTURE STATEMENT

We are a values-first company.

We believe culture isn't just a vibe—it's our root system.

We grow people. We grow products. We grow together.

*We lead with humility, act with courage,
and collaborate with care.*

We win with innovation, not ego.

We believe trust is earned, not assumed.

*We believe every person is a builder of
this culture—not just the leaders.*

We don't chase hype; we chase mastery.

*We speak with candor, act with integrity,
and never forget to laugh.*

*We are building a company where growth is the norm,
not the exception. And culture is our greatest product.*

This culture statement will be posted on our website, and we'll diligently teach and train our people on these "10 Culture Commandments," especially our hiring managers and teams so we align our hiring to our company culture.

WRITE YOUR OWN CULTURE STATEMENT (INSTRUCTIONS & TIPS)

Crafting your company culture statement isn't about getting the words perfect—it's about capturing your truth. It should be specific, aspirational, and most importantly—usable. Here's a step-by-step recipe:

Step 1: Reflect on the "Now"

- What does your current culture feel like?
- What behaviors do you reward and tolerate?
- What do your best people say about working here?

Step 2: Gather Inputs

- **Ask your leadership team:** What do we stand for?
- **Ask your team members:** What brings you pride? What needs to change?
- **Capture words, stories, and moments** that reflect your real culture.

Step 3: Write the "Preferred" Culture

- What kind of company do you want to become?
- If your culture was a product, what would the tagline be?
- **Finish this sentence:** "At our best, we…"

Step 4: Keep it Human

- Use conversational language—ditch the jargon.
- Avoid long-winded mission prose. This isn't a business plan.
- Aim for 6–10 lines and test it with your team.

Step 5: Make it a Living Thing

- Put it on the walls and in your decisions.
- Open team meetings with a value in action.
- Revisit it quarterly—culture evolves.

> **REMEMBER:** *Your culture statement isn't a poster— It's a promise.*

And the real magic? When your team starts living it before you even finish writing it.

CHAPTER 8

BUILDING A CULTURE OF EXCELLENCE

The VIBES Transformation at Work

By Monday, Ava walked into the office differently. She wasn't just leading. She was creating culture. And culture? That's what drives success.

She had a plan. Each day of the week would be dedicated to one part of VIBES.

SETTING THE VIBES PATH IN 5 DAYS: A CULTURE RESET

This wasn't just a reset. This was a revolution.

No more corporate fluff. No more posters with empty words. This was about action.

Ava stood in front of her team on Monday morning, staring at a group of people who had survived the storm, still standing but wary. Change was here, and this time, it was real.

Monday: V – Values & Beliefs – The Foundation of Leadership

The standing meeting felt different. Lighter. Clearer.

Ava stood in front of her team.

> *"We're not just fixing our business. We're rebuilding our culture. And that starts with our values."*

Instead of handing out a document with corporate jargon, she had each leader present a core value—but they couldn't just recite words from a slide.

They had to tell a story.

Megan, the new CRO, shared how she once stayed up all night helping a struggling sales rep land their first new deal—not because it was her job, but because that's what true leadership looks like.

John, the CFO, admitted he had almost quit—but he stayed because integrity mattered more than an easy way out.

Jenny, the CSO, shared how she finally spoke up to demand better customer support—because people, not just products, build loyalty.

Jane, the CTO, shared why customers are leaving, the product is over engineered and too hard to use —fixing the product to become user-friendly is within control.

By the end, the company's values weren't just words on a wall.

They were lived experiences.

People nodded. They weren't just hearing it. They were feeling it.

This was who they were now.

Tuesday: I – Interactions & Communication – The Transparency Rule

Ava set a new standard.

No more passive-aggressive emails.

No more hiding problems until it's too late.

No more fear of speaking up.

She introduced "Radical Listening"—a rule that leaders must listen for two full minutes before responding.

To prove it, she sat down with a team member, folded her arms, and said nothing for two minutes.

At first, people laughed.

Then they got uncomfortable.

Then they realized—oh crap, we actually have to listen.

By the end of the day, people were talking openly.

Because they finally knew they were being heard.

Ava didn't just want communication.

She wanted connection.

Wednesday: B – Behaviors & Rituals – Small Actions, Big Impact

Companies aren't built on grand moments.

They're built on small habits.

So, they restructured meetings—no more soul-sucking 90-minute time-wasters.

Every meeting had a clear purpose.

Every meeting was set in 25 min increments.[1] If a meeting could be an email, it was an email. If a meeting didn't need slides, no slides.

Then, Ava introduced a new ritual:

Every Friday, teams would celebrate small wins—not just big milestones.

Because success isn't one giant leap.

It's a series of small steps that no one notices—until they add up to something great.

By the end of the day, the team wasn't just working.

They were building momentum.

Companies aren't built on grand moments. They're built on small habits.

Thursday: E – Environment & Space – Designing for Focus

Ava walked into the office and saw the clutter.

Messy desks. Overloaded Slack channels. Too many meetings.

---

1   *Neuroscientists have scientifically proven that the average human/worker focus drops off significantly after 24-25 minutes. Meetings that last longer than 25 minutes are a waste of time. Let's face it, today's work culture is full of distractions, so 5-6 hours of deep quality work is all we're capable of delivering.*

So, she did a company-wide cleans.

Desks were cleared. If it didn't serve a purpose, it was gone. Noise was reduced. Open-office chaos? Not anymore. A "Focus Zone" was introduced—2 hours a day of no meetings, no Slack, just deep work.

At first, people grumbled.

By the end of the day? People felt lighter. More productive. More in control of their time.

They didn't realize how much mental space had been taken up by clutter— until it was gone.

Friday: S – Support & Leadership – Building a "People-First" Culture

Ava stood in front of her team, knowing this was the most important day of all.

"Success is a team sport. And culture is the real MVP."

She made leadership personal.

- Each executive was assigned a mentee. Leadership wasn't about titles. It was about building and lifting others up.
- Peer coaching became the new normal. No more silent competition— only collaboration.
- Psychological safety was the rule. No one was afraid to speak. No one was afraid to fail.

By the end of the day, something had shifted.

This wasn't just a workplace anymore.

This was a team.

Because at the end of the day, companies don't fail because of bad products.

They fail because of bad culture.

And Ava?

She was here to build a culture that lasted.

AVA'S REFLECTION – THE END OF THE WEEK, THE BEGINNING OF A LEGACY

Ava sat alone in her office on Friday evening, long after the last standing meeting of the week had ended. The office was quiet, safe from the hum of distant conversations and the occasional clack of a keyboard.

She leaned back in her chair, staring at the whiteboard still covered in handwritten values.

Integrity. Curiosity. Connection. Courage. Joy.

They weren't just words anymore. They were real. They were lived.

For the first time in her life, she wasn't chasing success.

She was building something that mattered.

For years, she thought leadership was about being the smartest person in the room. The one with the answers. The one who never doubted herself.

But that was a lie.

Leadership wasn't about knowing everything. It was about knowing your people.

It wasn't about having all the answers. It was about creating a space where people could find them together.

And for the first time, she didn't feel like she was carrying this company alone.

She had traveled across the world to find herself, find her values, find clarity.

And now, she realized—she had brought all of that back home.

This wasn't just about fixing a broken business.

It was about creating a culture that could withstand anything.

Because companies don't rise and fall on revenue alone.

They rise and fall on the people who build them.

And now?

She wasn't just running a company.

She was leading a movement.

She picked up her brass compass from the desk.

She held it in her hands, letting the weight of it settle in her palm.

She had flashbacks of her time in the Moroccan desert with Abdi.

For the first time in a long time, she wasn't lost.

She knew exactly where she was going.

She smiled, stood up, and walked out of her office.

Tomorrow, she would meet Bob.

SETTING THE STAGE – A CULTURE THAT LASTS

On Saturday morning, Ava rolled out of bed at 5:00 a.m. sharp.

It wasn't even a struggle anymore—it was a ritual.

She went through her morning routine, but today felt different.

Because today, she wasn't alone.

Her housemate, Camila, stretched beside her on the yoga mat, sipping green tea between deep breaths.

Now, it seemed Ava's self-care habits were rubbing off.

"Never thought I'd wake up before sunrise on a Saturday," Camila muttered, eyes half-open, hair in total disarray.

Ava smirked. "Welcome to a peaceful house culture."

THE COFFEE SHOP MEETING – ENTER BOB

Ava took the bullet train to Palo Alto and walked to her favorite coffee shop on University Avenue.

The scent of freshly brewed espresso, toasted bagels, and an unmistakable hint of over-caffeinated ambition filled the air.

She spotted Stanford students hunched over MacBooks, deep in their start-up pitches, coding sprints, or perceived crises.

It reminded her of herself.

She had been one of them—not just ambitious, but an overachiever who thrived on building things.

Now, she was here to **build something even bigger—**a culture that wouldn't crumble the moment she stepped away.

She ordered a small Brazilian dark roast, took a seat near the window, and pulled out her notebook.

It was time to reflect.

The past week has been transformational.

- She had fired a **fear-based leader** (bye, Catherine).
- She had **promoted the right people** (Megan and Jane were stepping up).
- She had **set clear values and expectations.**

And yet…

She needed more.

She had made good changes, but she wanted something that would last. Momentum could fade. Old habits could creep back.

She needed an expert. A guide. Someone who knew how to build cultures that could stand the test of time.

That's where Bob came in.

She had found him through her Stanford network—a guy who had taught culture at Stanford, written a best-selling book on the topic, and built his own firm specializing in cultural transformations and executive search.

Supposedly, Bob was the real deal.

Ava had imagined a corporate stiff in a navy-blue suit, armed with a 100-page PowerPoint presentation.

Instead—

Bob strolled in 10 minutes early, wearing a Patagonia vest, Allbirds sneakers, and holding his own travel coffee mug.

He oozed Silicon Valley energy—the kind of guy who had seen it all, failed spectacularly, learned from it, and came out wiser.

His presence was **a paradox—**like a tornado wrapped in the calmness of a still lake.

The kind of guy who could tear apart an executive team with brutal honesty and then hand them a plan to fix everything.

"You're Ava," he said, pulling up a chair. Not a question. A statement.

"And you're Bob," she replied, smiling.

"That's what they tell me." He took a long sip of his coffee, black as night.

Ava dove straight in.

She explained everything—her trip, her realizations, the values she had set, the leadership changes, the company reset.

Bob just listened.

Not the polite, obligatory listening.

The kind of listening that made you uncomfortable because you knew he was filing away every word and mentally highlighting every weak spot.

After a few minutes of silence, Ava finally asked, "So, what do you think?"

Bob leaned back and took another slow sip of coffee.

Then—he smirked.

BOB – THE MAN WHO'S SEEN IT ALL

"My first job out of college was inside sales," Bob started. "Terrible boss. High pressure. No training. The kind of job that either crushes you or makes you bulletproof."

Ava nodded. She had been there.

Bob continued, "I survived because I had a rule: Every challenge is a lesson. So, I didn't quit. I adapted."

He went on to explain how he built and trained his own sales team, which led to a job in HR, which led to 30 years of working inside some of the most demanding startups in Silicon Valley.

- He had hired thousands of people.
- He had fired just as many.
- He had built cultures from scratch—and watched them collapse when leaders screwed it up.

And now?

He was obsessed with fixing broken cultures.

"Culture isn't about perks, 'Thirsty Thursdays,' ping-pong tables, or unlimited PTO," Bob said before taking another aggressive sip of coffee. "It's about operating principles. It's about values that don't change when shit hits the fan. And if you don't deliberately design your culture, one will form on its own. And trust me—you probably won't like what you get."

Ava nodded. "I get that. I don't want a bunch of entitled startup bros running around demanding oat milk lattes and burning through VC money without accountability."

Bob smirked. "Exactly. So—first, we assess."

THE HARD TRUTH ABOUT CULTURE

Bob fired off his first question:

"Who owns culture?"

Ava: "I do."

Bob: "Correct. But can you run the entire company by yourself?"

Ava: "No, my leadership team should help. I also plan to hire a Chief Human Resources Officer (CHRO)."

Bob: "Most CEOs make a huge mistake by dumping culture on HR—and then starving them of budgets and authority. Culture starts with YOU. Your leadership team co-owns it. HR enables it. Believe me, I know it first-hand. Got it?"

Ava: "Got it."

Bob: "When did your company start faltering?"

Ava paused. "When I felt I lost control."

Bob grinned. "And what did you learn when you were lost?"

Ava smiled. "To fall back on my values."

Bob slammed his coffee cup down like he just won a poker hand. "YES! That's the foundation. But now, how do you get everyone else to believe in it?"

THE REALITY CHECK

Bob started pressing deeper.

Did you hire people based on values? Did you screen for cultural fit in interviews? Did you align your hiring process to the culture you wanted?

Ava hesitated.

She had never thought about it that way.

She had brilliant people on the team … but were they the right people?

Bob leaned in. "If you don't hire for culture, you will spend years trying to fix it."

Ava let that sink in.

She had already started the cleanup. She had fired Catherine. But who else wasn't aligned?

And more importantly—how would she prevent this problem in the future?

"If you don't hire for culture, you will spend years trying to fix it."

THE PLAN – A CULTURE THAT LASTS

Bob laid it out in **five steps:**

- **Step 1: Assess** – Run a science-based assessment using the 4-S Culture Model.
- **Step 2: Analyze** – Identify gaps between the current and ideal culture.

- **Step 3: Plan** – Define hiring and leadership strategies to reinforce culture.
- **Step 4: Execute** – Make the hard decisions. Hire. Fire. Align.
- **Step 5: Measure** – Track progress. Adjust. Build a culture that lasts.

Ava leaned back in her chair, exhaling slowly.

She had been burned by toxic leaders before.

It was time to fix that—permanently.

"Let's do it," Ava said.

Bob nodded. "Good. See you at your Monday standing meeting."

PART 2

CHAPTER 9

LEADERS ARE CULTURE BUILDERS

Ava sat in her office, arms crossed, staring at her whiteboard of chaos like it was some kind of crime scene investigation.

Sticky notes everywhere. Names. Titles. Open positions. And right in the middle, in giant, bold letters: "CMO???"

If she were still the old Ava, she'd be tempted to fill that question mark with any smooth talker who could throw around buzzwords like "synergy" and "brand activation."

But she wasn't that Ava anymore. This time, she needed to build a leadership team that wasn't just talented, but aligned.

Her generation—Millennials—had a completely different relationship with work than the ones before. They weren't looking to grind away in silence for stock options and burnout. They wanted meaning. Culture. A sense of purpose.[2]

And if Ava didn't set the culture from the boardroom to the coffee room to the Zoom room, someone else would.

That was not an option.

---

2   *Researchers have found out that the Millennial and Gen Z generations care more about purpose and culture than previous generations. So much so that if they don't feel part of the culture, they quit without having another job lined up.*

TEAM, MEET BOB

Monday morning. The first official meeting of the new era.

Ava walked into the standing leadership meeting with a different energy.

She wasn't here to manage tasks. She was here to change the game.

Bob and Michelle stood at the front of the room, coffee in hand.

Ava cut straight to the point. No fluff. No icebreakers.

"We've made some good progress," she said, looking around the room, "but we're nowhere near where we need to be. Culture is the foundation of our success, and today, we're going to fix it from the ground up."

She nodded at Bob.

Bob, wearing his usual Patagonia vest and the energy of a motivational coach who also moonlighted as a drill sergeant, took a step forward and grinned.

"Alright, let's cut to the chase," Bob said, sipping his coffee like it was jet fuel. "I've worked with Silicon Valley startups for 30 years. I've seen companies rise and fall, and guess what?"

He paused, letting the silence work its magic.

"The ones that fail—it's never because of a lack of talent." Bob paced, making sure to make eye contact with every leader in the room. "It's never because of bad product-market fit. It's never even about funding." He tapped his coffee mug like it held the secret to life itself.

"They fail because they let culture happen to them instead of creating it."

He let that sit.

"You can have the smartest engineers, the best salespeople, the most brilliant marketing minds," Bob continued. "But if the culture is toxic, it'll kill your company faster than an SEC investigation."

WHO OWNS CULTURE?

Bob scanned the room.

"Who owns culture?" he asked.

Silence. Then, John, the CFO, hesitated. "Uh … we do?"

The rest of the team nodded uncertainly, like students afraid of getting the answer wrong.

Bob grinned mischievously. "Let's put some energy into it." He turned up the volume like a drill instructor waking up a sleeping marine at bootcamp.

"WHO OWNS CULTURE?"

The team, startled, responded louder: "WE DO!"

Bob cupped his hand around his ear like a game show host hyping up a crowd. "Louder! I want the engineers to hear it! I want the Slack channels to FEEL it!"

"WE DO!" the entire team shouted.

Bob clapped his hands together. "Damn right you do. Now let's act like it."

The Brutal Truth—What the Employees Said

Bob clicked his remote, and a survey result popped up on the screen.

"Alright, here's the brutal truth," he said. "We surveyed 100 people at this company. Here's what they told us:"

- **They want clarity**. Right now, there's too much ambiguity on goals and expectations.
- **They crave psychological safety**. No more fear-based leadership (bye, Catherine).
- **They want extreme ownership**. No more finger-pointing. No more blame games.
- **They need better leadership**. Megan and Jenny? People follow them. But there are **gaps**. Huge gaps.

Bob turned and looked at the team.

"Any surprises?"

The team shook their heads.

"Good. That means we're being honest."

THE CULTURE ASSESSMENT—THE 4-S MODEL

Bob pulled up another slide. An illustration of a tree.

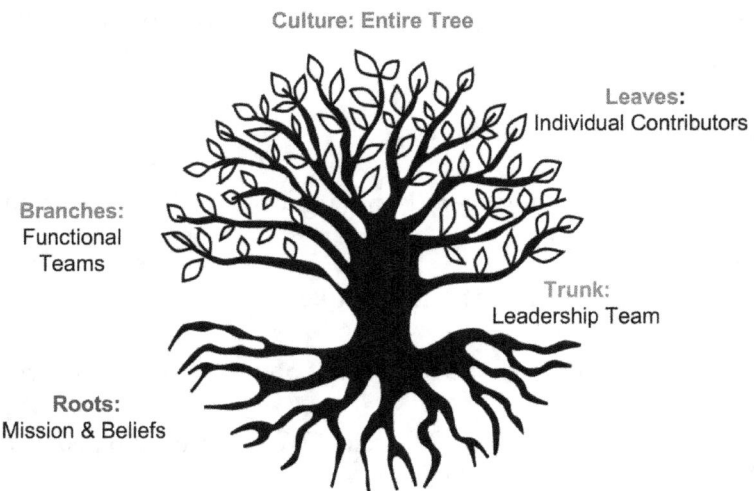

Illustration 1

"A company's culture," Bob began, "is like a thriving tree."

He pointed at the roots."These are your values, mission, and purpose. They anchor you through changing seasons."

Then the trunk. "This is leadership. The CEO and the executive team. You provide structure and direction."

Next, the branches. "These are your functions and managers. They extend outward, bringing different capabilities to the table."

And finally, the leaves. "These are your people. The energy. The movement. The life of the company."

Bob turned back to them. "Culture is the entire tree. And if one part is broken, the whole thing suffers."

He clicked to the next slide.

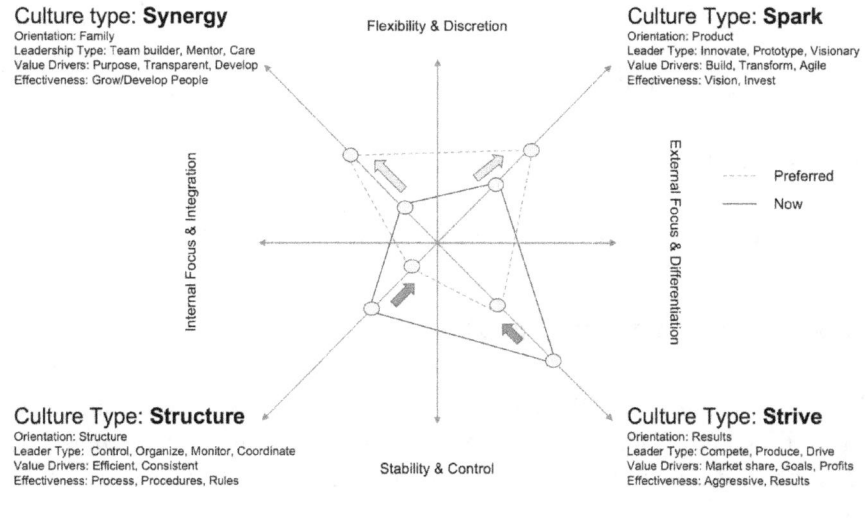

Illustration 2

"This is your culture assessment. Take a moment to absorb it."

The team stared at the results.

Ava already knew what they were about to see.

Bob took a sip of coffee and waited.

Then, Jenny, the CSO, spoke first. "We've been so focused on market share, we forgot about our people," she admitted. "It used to feel like a family. It hasn't for a long time."

John, the CFO, nodded. "What's weird is that we're equally strong in Structure and Spark."

Michelle, stepping in for the first time, nodded. "That's rare. What do you think it means?"

Morgan, the ex-CTO, rubbed his temples. "Feels like an identity crisis."

Megan sighed. "It's because of silos. Silos are culture killers."

Bob grinned. "Bingo."

Ava sat back, watching it all unfold.

For the first time, her team wasn't just reacting.

They were seeing the culture for what it was.

THE FIX—OWNERSHIP & ACTION

Just before diving into the tactical work, Bob stepped forward and gave Michelle a quick nod. She didn't need a cue—she was already moving, calm and deliberate, a quiet storm with a mission. In her hand was a stack of 5x7 index cards.

Without saying a word, she made a full lap around the room, handing one to each member of the leadership team. Some accepted theirs with curiosity, others with the kind of hesitation usually reserved for jury duty.

Once everyone had a card in hand, Michelle stood at the front and said, "On this card, I want you to write down the names of people in your organization who are not a cultural fit. No filter. Just honesty."

A few brows furrowed. One person coughed. Bob stepped up beside Ava and added, "And yes, this includes anyone. Even leaders. Especially leaders. This is about truth, not titles. Culture change doesn't happen unless we're willing to look in the mirror—and sometimes, the reflection needs a little reshuffling."

He looked around the room, steady and calm. "Take a minute or two to think and write the names and return the cards to Michelle. We need to move to our next exercise."

The room got quiet. Not tense—just real.

After a moment of quiet scribbling and sideways glances, Michelle went around the room again, collecting the cards like confessions in a secular cathedral.

Bob **broke them into teams.**

- **Jenny & Grace:** Fix Synergy—create an internal community again.
- **Morgan & Jane:** Fix Spark—make innovation a real priority.
- **Megan & Bob:** Fix Strive—make sales competitive, but ethical.
- **John & Michelle:** Fix Structure—clean up leadership accountability.

The teams scattered, huddling in corners of the room, grabbing whiteboards, talking fast. The energy shifted. This wasn't just another leadership offsite—this was the beginning of something.

Ava felt it.

Bob watched her for a moment, then walked over. "Ava," he said, motioning for her to stand. "Face me."

She got up, meeting his gaze. Bob had that rare ability to be both comforting and intense—like a grandfather who'd seen it all but could still take you in a wrestling match.

"I've reviewed the individual-level 4-S assessments on your leadership team," Bob said. "My experience tells me at least one, maybe more, won't make it with the new program."

Ava frowned. "Not because of skill?"

Bob shook his head. "No. Because some people resist change. Even good change. And when they resist? They either step up and transform—or they dig in and decay."

He paused. Then said, "Put your hands up. Palms out."

Ava hesitated but followed his instructions. Bob pressed his hands against hers—firm, steady pressure. Ava pushed right back with the same force.

"This," he said, eyes locked on hers, "is resistance."

Ava pressed harder. He didn't budge.

"Some of your team will push against the new culture. Not because they're bad people. But because change is uncomfortable. Some will lean in and inspire others. Some will quiet-quit and stall progress. Your job is to spot the difference."

Ava felt the weight of his words. If she let disengaged leaders sit in the system, they'd act like sand in an engine—grinding everything down.

Bob stepped back and dropped his hands. "You don't fix resistance. You let it reveal the people who don't belong."

Ava exhaled and nodded. She needed to watch carefully.

Because one or more of them wouldn't make it.

Ten minutes later, plans were in place.

Bob clapped his hands. "That's how you start a revolution."

Ava stood up. "This isn't just a meeting. This is our culture reset. We're not here to slap on quick fixes and hope for the best."

She pointed at the tree illustration.

"We are planting new roots, strengthening the trunk, growing the branches, and keeping our leaves alive."

The team nodded.

John looked at Ava. "This time, it's going to last, isn't it?"

Ava smiled. "This time, we're building a forest."

THE TURNING POINT – TEAM EXERCISE

Michelle's phone alarm chirped like a judgmental cricket—time was up.

The room buzzed with nervous energy. Everyone had spent the last ten minutes sketching out solutions but now came the moment of truth: presenting them.

Bob leaned against the conference table, cradling his ever-present coffee mug like a prized possession.

"Alright," he said, stretching his arms. "Who's up first? And don't make me pick, because I will—like a gym teacher eyeing the slowest runner."

Jenny and Grace stood up first.

SYNERGY – BRINGING THE FAMILY BACK TOGETHER

Jenny cleared her throat. "So, to fix Synergy, we need to stop acting like a collection of separate departments and start acting like a real team again. Here's what we propose:"

Hiring – We need to change our hiring practices to prioritize cultural fit as much as technical ability. No more 'brilliant jerks.' We'll evaluate hiring fit through structured behavioral interviews and track new hire performance and quarterly employee surveys (NPS) to measure alignment.

Transparent Communication – No more closed-door decisions. We'll hold weekly company-wide syncs where each function provides updates on progress, blockers, and new goals. Our measure? Live sentiment surveys[3] to track engagement levels and see if employees actually feel informed—or if they're just nodding to stay off the radar.

HR Upgrade – Our HR function is currently … well, underpowered. Our manager is great but too junior for what we need. Either we develop them into a strategic leader or hire someone new. Success here will be measured by leadership engagement scores and retention rates.

"People-First" Means "Customer-First" – Happy employees create happy customers. We'll measure success through customer NPS scores and retention levels. If employees feel supported and valued, we'll see that reflected in our customer relationships.

Bob nodded approvingly. "Good stuff. You're turning this place into a team, not a corporate *Hunger Games*."

SPARK – REIGNITING INNOVATION

Next up: Jane and Morgan.

---

3   *People tend to be more honest about their feelings during live company meetings and events. It's best to survey people during the meeting AND give them real-time results (for transparency) so they feel like they're being heard.*

Jane, newly appointed CTO and former Stanford tennis star, stood up confidently, flashing a no-nonsense look around the room. Morgan, less comfortable but visibly stepping up, followed her lead.

"Alright," Jane said, her voice strong and clear. "Here's how we fix Spark."

Hiring a Product Leader – "Morgan is a genius. But he's not a manager." (Morgan nodded in agreement.) "I will lead the engineers, but we need someone to lead the product managers. Ava will do that in the interim, but we'll need someone more permanent. We'll measure this by internal team engagement scores and product release efficiency."

Product Simplification – The "Churro Test" – "I've watched our product struggle in the market for one simple reason: it's confusing as hell. That stops now. Our new standard: a non-engineer should be able to deploy our product before finishing a churro. If it fails the Churro Test, we redesign it. We'll measure this through time-to-deployment data and usability scores."

Morgan, now warming up, added:

Breaking Down Silos – "Product, Sales, Marketing, and Finance must collaborate. No more 'us vs. them.' We'll have a weekly cross-functional sync where goals overlap. Our measure? Shared OKRs and accountability across teams."

Project Clean-Up – "I've hired people who are brilliant but impossible to work with," Morgan continued. "I'll fix that. Either they align or they leave. We'll measure this by tracking team sentiment scores and reduction in unnecessary project backlogs."

Bob grinned. "Love it. The 'Churro Test' is ridiculous, but I'm all in. If it takes longer to deploy than eating fried dough, we've failed."

STRIVE – COMPETING THE RIGHT WAY

Megan strode up like she was about to pitch to a major investor.

"Let's be real," she said. "We've been too aggressive in chasing deals without thinking about long-term partnerships. We need to fix how we Strive."

Sales Process Revamp – "We're moving from transactional selling to value-based partnerships. No more 'land the deal, dump the mess on Customer Success.' Our measure? Sales conversion rates + long-term customer retention."

Partnerships Matter – "Product needs to align with Sales to ensure customers get what they actually need. Marketing needs to generate qualified leads, not just traffic. And Customer Success needs a direct line to Sales for real-time feedback. Our measure? Cross-team success KPIs + churn reduction."

Sales Effectiveness – "We're bringing in a Sales Ops specialist to track conversion rates and clean up inefficiencies. Any underperformers will go on a performance plan. Our measure? Increased sales velocity and deal close rate."

Freemium Model Test – "We'll test offering a lighter version of our product for 60 days to drive leads. If we see a conversion rate above 25%, we'll expand it. If not, we kill it."

Bob raised his coffee mug. "That's how you sell without selling your soul. Approved."

STRUCTURE – THE BACKBONE OF THE COMPANY

Last up: John.

John, for the first time in months, actually looked excited.

"Alright," he said. "Here's how we fix Structure."

Funding – "We have five term sheets, and we'll push for at least five more. I need a new pitch deck from each function lead to give investors a clear picture. Our measure? Securing funding with at least four to five years of runway."

Finance & Ops Alignment – "Finance has been on an island. That stops now. We'll hold weekly alignment meetings to ensure spending priorities match strategic goals. Our measure? Clear budget accountability + reduced unnecessary expenditures."

HR Upgrade – "I admit it: I've treated HR like an afterthought. That changes. We're budgeting for a real HR leader in our next funding round. Our measure? HR leadership hire within six months + strategic people initiatives in place."

Burn Rate Management – "No more reckless spending. We're cutting unnecessary expenses by 20% in three months. Layoffs are a last resort, but we're getting lean and smart. Our measure? Cash burn reduction + financial sustainability."

Bob leaned in. If you pull this off, you won't just be a CFO, you'll be a strategic architect."

John grinned. "That's the goal."

CULTURE CLEAN-UP – THE HARD PART

Michelle stood at the front of the room, holding the stack of 5x7 cards like a deck of uncomfortable truths.

"These," she said, fanning them out slightly, "are the names you each wrote down—people who don't align with the culture we're building. This wasn't about blame or shame. It was about clarity. Culture isn't just about what you say—it's about what you tolerate."

She paused and looked around the room. "The good news? No one wrote each other's names. This leadership team is aligned. The tough news? Every single one of you wrote down at least three people who no longer fit."

A hush settled in. It wasn't anger—it was the gravity of the moment.

Megan spoke first.

"Some sales reps don't fit our new model. We'll need a plan to replace them while keeping regional coverage. We'll have a transition plan in place within 60 days."

Ava nodded. "Marketing needs a full clean-up. We'll cut spending by 30% and rebuild a smaller but effective team."

Jane looked at Morgan. "Product and Engineering need restructuring. We'll finalize team changes in 60 days."

John leaned back. "Some Engineering managers are nightmares to work with. If we fix that, we fix a lot. We'll track culture impact on team productivity."

Bob smiled. "Now you're thinking like builders."

Michelle said, "Remember, the fastest way to change the culture is to change the people. Culture is the company's personality. If someone's values do not align with ours, they do not fit in, period. You cannot rationalize keeping them because they have the brains of Einstein. It's unhealthy for those folks to stay at the company, because they are not truly happy and it hurts the organization in the process."

Ava stood, looking at the tree illustration.

"We are planting new roots," she said. "This company will not just survive. It will grow."

Bob lifted his mug. "That's the spirit. Now let's get to work."

Bob: Wow, that was intense, and I need more coffee!

THE NEW STRUCTURE: TEAMS WITH PURPOSE

Ava divided the company into **three essential pillars**:

1. Product Team (Middle Office – The Architects)

> **MISSION:** *Design, develop, and deploy products that customers don't just like—but love.*

No more building in a vacuum. Customer-first, not feature-first. Design what people can't live without.

The Leadership Fix:

- Morgan was a technical genius but a terrible manager. Instead of forcing him to lead, Ava gave him a Technical Fellow role—a respected individual contributor who sets the technical direction.

- The Product Leadership gap needed to be filled ASAP. Bob and Michelle's executive search firm would handle this with a culture-first approach.

2. Go-To-Market Team (Front Office – The Closers)

> **MISSION:** *Not just to sell. To build lifelong partners.*

Sales, marketing, and customer success must work together. No more departmental silos—everyone owns the customer experience. Customers will now be called "Partners" because we are in it for the long haul.

The Leadership Fix:

- Megan, the new CRO, was an absolute rockstar. Ava needed to set her up for success.

- The CMO role was vacant. The wrong hire would kill momentum. They needed a marketing leader who understood storytelling, brand, and partner experience.

- Jenny, the CSO, was finding her voice. Ava would mentor her to own her leadership presence.

3. General & Administrative (Back Office – The Enablers)

> **MISSION:** *Build the infrastructure for scale without becoming a corporate bureaucracy.*

- G&A should support the business, not slow it down.
- No bloated leadership teams or wasted resources.
- Operate like a scrappy startup but think like an enterprise.

The Leadership Fix:

- John, the CFO, had recommitted. He was laser-focused on securing the next funding round.
- They desperately needed a CHRO. Someone who understood that culture is built, not assumed.
- No more "HR as a compliance function." They needed an HR leader who built high-performance cultures, not just policy enforcers.

FINAL TAKEAWAYS – THE VIBES REVOLUTION AT WORK & HOME

- Culture isn't about words. It's about actions.
- Fulfillment is a lifestyle, not a goal.
- Excellence comes from alignment—values, communication, behavior, environment, and support.
- The best leaders don't just lead—they build systems where others can lead too.
- VIBES is more than a framework—it's the foundation of a fulfilling, high-performing life.

Ava took a deep breath.

She wasn't chasing happiness hits anymore.

She was building something real.

And this?

This was just the beginning.

IMPORTANT NOTE FROM THE AUTHOR

Ava's journey—both personal and professional—isn't a straight road. It never is. Bob's job wasn't to hand her a magic formula or a shortcut to success. His job was to give her the tools, the map, and the mindset to keep moving forward.

Some people take the easy road—they avoid discomfort, dodge challenges, and hope for smooth sailing. But the ones who choose the harder path, who keep forging ahead no matter how rough it gets? They build grit, resilience, and wisdom that no shortcut can provide.

Let's get one thing straight: there are no life hacks for this thing called life. There are no cheat codes. No "3 Easy Steps to Success" nonsense. If there were, we'd all be billionaires with six-pack abs and unshakable confidence.

The only way forward? Chop wood. Carry water.

There's an old Zen saying:

"Even monkeys fall from the tree."

Think about it. Even the best, most experienced, most seemingly invincible fall sometimes. It's part of the game.

There's another saying that follows it:

"Fall down seven times, get up eight."

That's Ava's story. That's all of our stories.

Ava and her team made their own decisions. Were they perfect? No. But as long as they carried the right set of values, they would continue to learn, adapt, and grow. That's the only real guarantee in life.

So, as you go on your own journey, ask yourself:

- Are you avoiding the hard path, or embracing it?
- Are you chasing shortcuts, or putting in the work?
- Are you afraid to fall, or are you ready to get back up—again and again?

Because, in the end, the journey is the reward.

CHAPTER 10

CULTURE IN MOTION

ANOTHER NOTE FROM THE AUTHOR

Before reading on, I suggest you grab a highlighter, notebook, and your favorite writing utensil. This chapter is packed with tested ideas, what I call golden nuggets. These nuggets aren't just theories—they come from three decades of hands-on experience, trial and error, and, frankly, a whole lot of failure. **All of these scenarios happened in real life.**

Some of these ideas might feel unconventional, even radical. And that's the point. If you want real change, you have to be bold enough to experiment. So, as you read, mark the concepts that challenge you, that make you pause, that ignite a spark. Because at the end of the day, culture isn't about what you say—it's about what you do.

Now, let's get back to work.

FAST FORWARD: SIX MONTHS LATER

Ava woke up charged. Not just her phone—her entire being.

Monday morning. September in San Francisco. The kind of crisp, golden morning that made the city look like it had been Photoshopped for a tech company's homepage.

After her morning ritual with Camila—who had, to Ava's amusement, fully adopted her meditation and tea-drinking habits—she set off for work. A 15-minute walk, just enough time to mentally organize her day and admire the city's unique chaos: A mix of hoodies and designer suits, scooters weaving through traffic like over-caffeinated bees, and the ever-present scent of fresh sourdough and … was that weed? Probably.

She was seeing Bob today. And she had a lot to report.

REUNION AT THE OFFICE

As she entered the lobby of her building, there he was.

Bob.

Blue Patagonia vest? Check. T-shirt and khakis? Check. Matching Allbirds? Of course. Travel mug? Like a knight's sword.

Their eyes met, and Bob cracked a huge, warm grin. Ava didn't hesitate. She walked straight up to him and wrapped him in a hug like he was her long-lost dad.

Bob squeezed back—with just enough pressure to say, *I missed you too,* and just enough extra seconds to remind Ava *he meant it.*

"Long time, no see," Ava said, stepping back.

Bob chuckled. "I didn't expect a hug, but I'm a hugger myself. And I love San Francisco this time of year. I used to live here—September was always the best."

"Because it's the only month without fog?" Ava teased.

"Exactly."

She motioned for him to follow her upstairs. As they entered her office, Bob placed a small bag on her desk.

Bob grinned. "Got you something."

Ava peered inside. A bag of Brazilian dark roast coffee.

Her smile widened. "I love Brazilian coffee. How did you know?"

Bob took a sip from his ever-present travel mug. "Because you have good taste."

Ava laughed.

Bob leaned forward, eyes twinkling. "Alright, kid. Let's hear it. How's the tree?"

CULTIVATING EXCELLENCE

Ava leaned back in her chair, exhaling deeply. She had learned so much.

"Okay, where do I start? Let me start with culture, then leadership, then the functional updates," she said. "And we'll close with questions, if any."

Bob nodded approvingly.

She continued, "You told me once that what gets measured, gets managed, and what doesn't? Gets neglected. We got down to action on the 4-S's. Every leader presented their action plan—with metrics. No guessing. No empty-based decision-making. We tracked everything."

Bob raised an eyebrow. "And?"

Ava grinned. "It's working." She pulled up a slide on her screen.

A tree. The same one Bob had shown them six months ago.

- **Roots (Values, Mission, Purpose):** Clear, written, reinforced.
- **Trunk (Leadership):** Stronger. Decision-making aligned, not chaotic.
- **Branches (Departments):** Interconnected. No more silos.

- **Leaves (People):** Engaged, energized, growing.

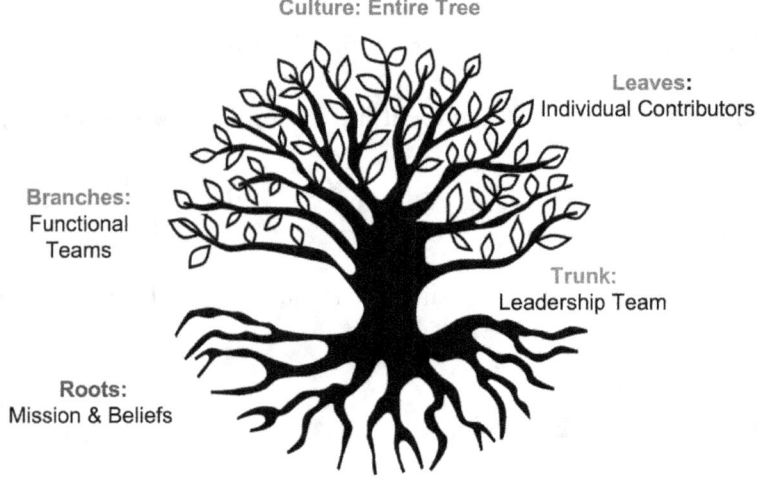

Illustration 3

Bob leaned in. "Damn. Look at that tree. It's thriving."

Ava smiled. "Because we didn't leave it to chance."

THE LEADERSHIP SHIFT

Bob sat back. "What was the hardest lesson?"

Ava didn't hesitate.

"That culture requires cultivation. If you let it grow wild, it doesn't turn into a Redwood— it turns into a tangled mess of weeds."

She took a breath.

"I had to actively shape this culture. Every day. And I had to become a better leader to do it."

Ava's Leadership Lessons

Ava clicked to the next slide.

Five Hard-Won Lessons on Leadership:

- **Build Trust with Small Wins:** Trust isn't built with grand gestures—it's built with consistent, reliable actions over time. Show up. Follow through. Repeat.
- **Create Psychological Safety:** If people are scared to speak up, innovation dies. We made it safe to take risks, make mistakes worth making, fail, and learn. Fail forward.
- **Lead by Listening, Not Commanding:** The best leaders ask, listen, and empower. I stopped talking first and started listening more.
- **Find & Nurture Mentors:** I surrounded myself with people who'd walked this path before. You included, Bob.
- **Give More Than You Take:** The best cultures aren't built on transactions, but on generosity. We started mentoring internally. "Paying it forward" became an expectation.

Bob nodded slowly. "You've been doing the work."

Ava smiled. "Every damn day."

Bob took another sip of coffee. "So, what's next?"

Ava grinned. "We keep growing the forest."

Bob laughed. "That's my girl."

The culture wasn't just holding.

It was thriving.

THE CULTURE TREE—VIBES IN ACTION

Ava grabbed a marker and walked up to the whiteboard.

Bob leaned back in his chair. "Is the tree thriving, or are we still pulling weeds?"

Ava smiled. "Not only is it thriving—it's bearing fruit."

She tapped the roots.

V – Values: Our North Star

Ava circled the roots.

"This was the foundation. If we didn't get this right, everything else would collapse."

- Values aren't just posters on the wall—they're the GPS for every decision.
- Every meeting starts with a values check-in. Someone shares a real example of how they used a value in a decision.
- Hiring, firing, promotions—everything is tied to values. If you don't align, you don't belong.

Ava turned to Bob. "I start every morning reviewing my personal values as affirmations. It gives me clarity and focus. Now, my leaders do the same."

Bob nodded. "And? Have people resisted?"

Ava chuckled. "Oh yeah. Some thought it was corny at first. But when we started making decisions that weren't just about profits, but about who we wanted to be—they got it. Now, it's second nature."

Values aren't just posters on the wall—they're the GPS for every decision.

I – Interactions & Communication: No More Corporate Nonsense

Ava **moved to the trunk.**

"This is where we stopped tolerating BS."

- No passive-aggressive emails. Say what you mean.
- Meetings capped at 25 minutes. If you need longer, you're unprepared.
- If we smell drama or politics, we call it out. Immediately.

She pointed at Bob. "You taught me: 'Listen with your whole mind and heart.' Now, it's a rule here."

Bob grinned. "And?"

Ava replied. "Turns out, when people actually listen, problems get solved faster."

B – Behaviors & Rituals: Shaping Identity

Ava traced the **branches.**

"We knew that culture wasn't just about words. It's about what we do every single day."

- **Step 1:** Identify people who don't fit. Give them 30 days to align—or leave.
- **Step 2:** Hire people who actively embody our values. We don't 'train' values.
- **Step 3:** Create feedback loops. A confidential Slack channel for calling out toxic behaviors.

Bob chuckled. "And you ditched happy hours?"

Ava nodded. "Instead, managers take their teams for coffee, one-on-one. Real conversations, no forced networking."

She smirked. "Also, we have a pickleball league. Sales and Customer Success are cutthroat."

Bob grinned. "Let me guess—Sales talks a big game?"

Ava rolled her eyes. "Nonstop. But Customer Success wins more than they'd like to admit."

E – Environment & Space: Designing for Focus

Ava pointed at the leaves.

"This was one of the most immediate changes."

- **Focus Zones:** Two hours a day—no Slack, no emails, no meetings. Just deep work.
- **Decluttering Everything:** Cleaned up laptops, file structures, and Slack channels.
- **Physical Space:** Music in one section, silence in another. No more distractions.

"But Bob," she said, lowering her voice, "the real shift wasn't just physical. It was emotional."

She met his eyes.

"We created a circle of safety. You told me people can't thrive if they don't feel safe."

Bob nodded.

"So now, at our leadership dinners, we share our highs and lows. And some of those lows get deep. The leaders who weren't comfortable with that? They left."

S – Support & Leadership: Building Future Leaders

Ava tapped the trunk again.

"This part? This is where we won."

- Every leader has at least two mentees. If they can't find one, they hire one.
- Mentees shadow leaders in real-time. No theory—just action.
- We share leadership skills openly. No hoarding knowledge.

She took a deep breath.

"I've personally created a circle of safety for my leaders. I tell them every single day—'I got your back, just go for it.'"

Bob leaned back, smiling. "And?"

Ava grinned.

"There's so much oxytocin in this company, it's ridiculous."

THE HARD TRUTH—NOT EVERYONE MADE IT

Ava's expression turned serious.

"The hardest part? Letting people go."

She sighed.

"We lost John, our ex-CFO. He was a good person, but he couldn't adapt. He second-guessed the culture shift. He resisted change. He was too rigid in his ways."

Bob nodded. "You don't build culture with the wrong people, or worse, tolerate them for a long time."

Ava exhaled. "I know. And I made peace with it. Because we are a values-based culture now. We don't make exceptions."

She tapped the whiteboard again.

"Bob, every function in this company serves our values. That's the new rule."

THE FUNCTIONAL TEAM REVAMP REPORT

Ava picked up a marker and turned back to Bob.

"Alright, let's start with the backbone of the company—the G&A team." She circled the trunk of the Culture Tree on the whiteboard.

Bob sipped his coffee. "Ah, the unsung heroes. The engine room."

Ava nodded. "More like the department that was drowning in red tape and micromanagement."

G&A: Breaking Free from Bureaucracy

"The Finance, Legal, People, IT, and Admin teams are supposed to **enable the company**—not slow it down. But under John's leadership, it was the opposite."

Bob raised an eyebrow. "Ah, yes. John's 'Structure-First' philosophy."

Ava nodded. "Look, I appreciate structure. But when it chokes innovation? It's a problem. I saw it firsthand when we worked on our funding round. I was drowning in John's analysis paralysis. I had to double my effort just to push things through."

"We parted ways amicably. He'd do great in a slow-moving, predictable environment. This wasn't it."

Bob nodded. "And lesson learned?"

Ava leaned against her desk. "I let the board influence me too much when we hired John. I didn't probe for culture fit. That won't happen again."

Bob grinned. "I assume you need help finding a transformational CFO now?"

Ava laughed. "Oh, absolutely. I need a partner, not an anchor. Unfortunately, John hired submissive people who were severely micromanaged, and I am not sure how many of them would fit in. We need a new perspective and leadership; this topic deserves a separate focused meeting."

Bob raised his coffee. "Done. Now tell me about your fundraising."

Ava grinned like a kid on Christmas morning. "We closed $125 million. And the best part? I still own more than half the company and retain voting control. Investors bet on our culture, vision, and execution. Not just the product."

Bob whistled. "Damn. You're buying the next coffee."

Ava smirked. "Gladly."

The People Team—From HR to Strategic Growth

Bob leaned forward. "And Jesse? How's she doing?"

Ava clapped her hands together. "Jesse is a freaking rockstar. And, by the way—thank you for talking me out of hiring a CHRO."

Bob nodded. "Told you—you needed a VP who could execute, not a theorist or armchair CHRO."

Ava beamed. "Jesse came in knowing exactly what she was getting into. She shadowed me and the leadership team before she accepted the job and then came back with a Programmatic People Strategy (PPS)."

Bob grinned. "Smart. What did she focus on?"

Ava walked over to the whiteboard and drew a table.

THE PEOPLE TEAM'S 4 PILLARS

Ava pulled out her market and drew a chart on the whiteboard. (see chart 1)

Ava: We want to keep things simple, so we are going to focus on our 4 People Pillars:

1. **Hiring:** feeding the right people and talent to our culture.

2. **Performing:** people are hungry for feedback and want to grow their careers.

3. **Paying:** align our compensation to growth.

4. **Learning:**- as you taught me, Bob, growing people are engaged people.

Function	Philosophy	Action Items	Metrics
Hiring	Practice our ABCs—Hire for Abilities, Behaviors, and Culture.	Pre-hire culture assessment. Structured interviews focusing equally on ABCs. Hire for potential, not just experience. Hiring managers own the process—People team enables.	60-day hiring & new hire feedback.
Performing	Growth, not just performance. People must be actively developing to stay in our culture.	Monthly feedback cycles. Replace "Performance Management" with "Growth Management." Managers own development—People team enables.	80% in the Green Zone 20% in the Blue Zone. 0% in the Orange Zone (See illustration 4)

Function	Philosophy	Action Items	Metrics
Paying	Pay for Growth. Reward and retain those with a growth mindset.	Transparent salary ranges. Market pay at the 50th percentile. Double equity for new hires & employees vested >50%.	>90% retention of high performers.
Learning	We don't just hire growth-minded people—we grow them.	Everyone has a mentor/coach. Every employee gets a customer or prospect visit.	>50% in Green Zone >50% in Blue Zone 0% in Orange Zone

Table 1

Bob studied the table, nodding. "This is gold."

Ava grinned. "It's working."

Bob sipped his coffee. "Tell me the biggest win so far."

Ava didn't hesitate. "We hire differently. We fire differently. And now? We promote differently."

Bob raised an eyebrow. "Meaning?"

Ava leaned in. "We only promote people who actively develop others. If you're not mentoring or coaching, you don't move up. We also shifted our hiring to local talent, especially at junior levels because they learn by being under the same roof as their managers and team members. Osmosis is a beautiful thing."

Bob's smile widened. "That's how you scale a strong culture."

Ava tapped the board. "Bob, we're not just a company anymore. We're a place where people come to grow."

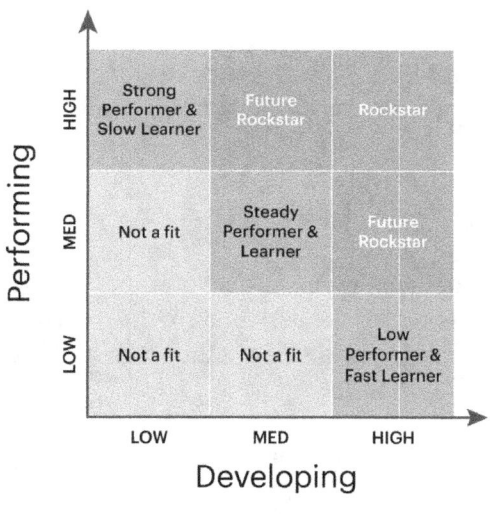

Illustration 4

GO-TO-MARKET TEAM REVAMP—BUILDING A GROWTH MACHINE

Ava tapped the whiteboard with a fresh marker, ready to dive into the next section. "Alright, Bob. Let's talk about the customer-facing teams—Sales, Marketing, and Customer Success."

Bob grinned. "Ah yes, the teams that either make you rich or make you question every life choice."

Ava laughed. "Exactly. But this time? We've got it right."

She underlined a name on the board. CHLOE – CGO (Chief Growth Officer).

Ava turned to Bob. "First of all, thank you for pushing me to change the title from CMO to CGO."

Bob nodded. "Words matter. Marketing doesn't exist in a vacuum. Growth is the job."

Ava smiled. "Right? The old marketing team burned cash like it was Monopoly money, with no measurable results. But Chloe? Chloe is a different breed."

Bob raised an eyebrow. "Tell me about her."

Ava leaned forward. "She's an operator. Not some 'brand guru' who throws money at ads and hopes for the best. She's in the trenches. She talks to customers, works with Sales, and understands how marketing actually converts to revenue."

Bob took a sip of coffee. "Sounds like you set her up for success."

Ava grinned. "We did. And I followed the process you drilled into me."

Bob leaned back. "Alright then, let's hear it. Walk me through how you hired her."

"Words matter. Marketing doesn't exist in a vacuum. Growth is the job."

THE GROWTH HIRING PLAYBOOK

Ava grabbed the marker and listed the steps on the board.

1. **Video Screen with Fully Vetted Candidates:** We only interviewed top-tier candidates who passed the **ABC test** (Abilities, Behaviors, Culture fit).

2. **Structured In-Person Interviews:** Three finalists met with our interview team. No casual coffee chats—structured questions, clear scoring.

3. **Round Table Discussion:** The interviewers compared notes, debating strengths and weaknesses.

4. **"Day in the Life" Experience:** Finalists spent a full day with us, interacting with the team to see if they truly fit.

5. **Strategic Presentation Challenge:** We gave candidates real inputs and had them present a strategy to see them in action before hiring.

6. **Reference Checks & Backchanneling:** We personally called references and did discreet backchannel checks to make sure they were the real deal, not just good interviewers.

7. **Closing the Top Candidate:** No dragging our feet. Once we found the one, we closed immediately.

8. **Onboarding & Cultural Immersion:** We didn't just throw Chloe into the deep end. She ramped up with our values as her guide.

Bob studied the board, then smiled. "Damn, you memorized it."

Ava grinned. "I learned from the best."

Bob nodded. "So, is she delivering?"

Ava crossed her arms. "Bob, in three months, Chloe has generated more qualified leads than the old CMO did in eighteen. And with half the budget."

Bob whistled. "Damn."

Ava smirked. "She's not just some ad-spending machine. She goes on sales calls, understands our buyer personas, and actually gets the product. She's educating us, not the other way around."

Bob leaned forward. "How's the team responding?"

Ava grinned. "Megan, our CRO, loves her. They're both on the same compensation plan—so their incentives are aligned."

Bob nodded approvingly. "Ah, no unhealthy friction between Sales and Marketing. That's a first."

Ava laughed. "Right? No more finger-pointing. Just joint and extreme accountability."

Bob took another sip of coffee, clearly impressed. "Alright, so what's next?"

THE NEXT PHASE – SCALING THE GO-TO-MARKET MACHINE

Ava underlined the next steps on the board.

- **Sales & Marketing Alignment:** No more leads that go nowhere. We built a joint lead-scoring model between Sales and Marketing, so only high-quality prospects go to the sales team.
- **Revenue Intelligence:** Chloe introduced a data-driven approach to track what's actually working, so we double down on high-converting channels.
- **Customer Success Integration:** We stopped treating Customer Success as an afterthought. Now, they're involved before the sale even closes to ensure a smooth transition.
- **Outbound Experimentation:** We tripled our outreach efforts, but we do it smart—targeted, value-based, and deeply personalized.
- **Community-Led Growth:** We're leveraging our happiest customers to refer new business. Chloe's team built a referral engine that's already paying off.

Bob leaned back, clearly impressed. "You didn't just fix the team. You re-built the engine."

Ava nodded. "Marketing, Sales, and Customer Success are finally rowing in the same direction."

Bob smiled. "And the best part?"

Ava grinned. "We're not just selling. We're building a movement."

Bob stood up and stretched. "So, if I were to sum this up…"

Ava crossed her arms, waiting.

Bob nodded.

- You hired the right leader.
- You built a hiring playbook that ensures alignment.
- You created a revenue machine instead of a marketing black hole.
- Your teams are finally collaborating instead of fighting.
- And … you actually like your Go-to-Market function now.

SALES, MARKETING & CUSTOMER SUCCESS – THE THREE MUSKETEERS

Ava laughed. "Damn right. We don't have any excuses for failure."

She underlined three names on the board.

Megan (CRO), Chloe (CGO), and Jenny (CSO).

"They're like the Three Musketeers, Bob. They're not generals sitting on a hill, watching the battle unfold. They lead from the front."

Bob raised an eyebrow. "Meaning?"

Ava smirked. "They go into the trenches. They attend prospect and client meetings, but they don't take over. They provide just enough air support and let their teams shine under the spotlight."

Bob nodded. "That's leadership."

Ava continued.

- **Megan (CRO):** Revamped the Sales org by territory and industry. Leveraged sales analytics with Chloe to build a repeatable sales play-book. Sales reps are finally hitting their numbers.
- **Jenny (CSO):** Transformed. She went from quiet and hesitant to a powerhouse. How? Stand-up comedy classes. No joke. It taught her confidence, adaptability, and humor.
- **Chloe (CGO):** Marketing and Sales are fully aligned. No more random spending. Everything is measured, tracked, and optimized.

We have strong **Synergy** here.

Bob leaned back in his chair, jaw slightly open. "Jenny is taking stand-up comedy classes?"

Ava nodded. "One day, during our walk-and-talk 1:1, I asked her what changed. She told me, 'I'm naturally an introvert, but I love to learn. And that means getting out of my comfort zone. So, I signed up for stand-up comedy. It rewired my mindset. Now, I love taking risks.'"

Bob shook his head, grinning. "Damn. Who would've thought?"

Ava stated. "Exactly. That's what happens when you create a culture of growth. People reinvent themselves."

Bob nodded, grinning. "Alright. What's next?"

Ava pointed at the next section on the whiteboard. "Product. We're about to rebuild it from the ground up."

Bob's eyes twinkled. "Now this … is gonna be fun."

PRODUCT TEAM—FROM CHAOS TO INNOVATION

Ava turned back to the whiteboard and wrote one word in giant letters.

INNOVATION.

Then, she drew three circles beneath it:

- Product Management
- Engineering
- Research

"Bob, six months ago, this function was a dysfunctional mess. If chaos and confusion had a love child, it would have been our Product team."

Bob chuckled. "Oh, I remember. It was like watching a band where each musician played their songs in different key signatures ... at full volume."

Ava nodded. "Exactly. No one was in sync. Customers were frustrated. We had no system, no cohesion. And worst of all? Our product was a nightmare to deploy."

Bob raised an eyebrow. "How'd you fix it?"

PRODUCT MANAGEMENT—THE CHURRO TEST REVOLUTION

Ava underlined Product Management. "This one? I took over personally."

Bob leaned forward. "Oh, this is gonna be good."

Ava smirked.

"I ripped everything apart and built it back from the ground up. I asked one simple question:

Why do customers struggle with deployment?"

Bob nodded. "The right question."

Ava continued. "We realized usability was a disaster. If our engineers couldn't set up our product faster than eating a foot-long churro, we fail."

Bob laughed. "The Churro Test. You actually did it?"

Ava grinned. "Oh, we went all in. We built our entire usability framework around speed and simplicity."

Bob sipped his coffee. "And?"

Ava pointed at the board.

- **Hired a UI/UX expert:** Someone who thinks in user flow, not just features.
- **Created a customer feedback loop:** Engineers now get real-time usability feedback.
- **Redesigned onboarding:** The new setup takes minutes, not hours.

Ava crossed her arms. "Our latest customer NPS (Net Promoter Score) just jumped 40 points."

Bob whistled. "That's insane."

Ava grinned. "And I brought in Ali to lead Product Management. He's one of my mentees."

Bob raised an eyebrow. "You put him through the hiring gauntlet?"

Ava nodded. "Oh, brutal. But he passed with flying colors."

ENGINEERING—FROM LONE WOLVES TO A CHAMPIONSHIP TEAM

Ava circled Engineering on the whiteboard and underlined it twice.

"This team? Total rebuild. And Jane? She made it happen."

Bob leaned back, taking a slow sip of his coffee. "Let me guess … big egos had to go."

Ava scowled. "Oh yeah. Some of these engineers thought they were gods of the keyboard. They wrote brilliant code but couldn't work together to save their lives."

Bob nodded knowingly. "And Jane? She cracked the whip?"

Ava laughed. "Oh, Jane didn't just crack the whip—she set the whole damn thing on fire."

Bob raised an eyebrow.

Ava leaned in. "Look, Jane is tough as hell. She was a Stanford tennis star—ranked top 20 before she blew out her knee. That kind of competitive fire? It doesn't go away. She brings that same intensity to Engineering."

Bob smirked. "Let me guess—she swears like a sailor?"

Ava grinned. "Oh, she drops more f-bombs than a Tarantino movie. But that's why they respect her. She doesn't sugarcoat anything, and she's scary smart. She didn't just clean up Engineering—she rebuilt or I better say 're-engineered' its DNA."

Bob chuckled. "She sounds like a force of nature."

Ava nodded. "She is. And honestly? We needed her."

THE 2004 OLYMPIC LESSON

Bob leaned forward. "Ever heard of the 2004 U.S. Olympic Basketball Team?"

Ava shook her head.

Bob smiled. "Let me tell you a story."

"In 1992, the US built the Dream Team—the greatest NBA players ever. Jordan. Magic. Bird. They dominated. They won gold. Destroyed every opponent."

Ava nodded. "And in 2004?"

Bob smirked. "They assembled another team full of superstars. But this time? They lost. To Argentina."

Ava's jaw dropped. "Wait. Argentina beat the US?"

Bob nodded. "The 1992 team played as a unit. The 2004 team played like individuals. Talent alone isn't enough. You need teamwork."

Ava shook her head. "Wow. That's exactly what happened in Engineering."

Bob chuckled. "So, what'd Jane do?"

Jane's Game Plan—No More Lone Wolves

Ava crossed her arms.

"Jane fired the prima donnas. We had all the talent, but no teamwork. Our engineers were solo acts, and we needed a conductor."

Bob raised an eyebrow. "And how's Jane doing now?"

Ava grinned. "Jane is the right leader. She's full of grit, respected, and doesn't take shit from anyone."

Bob inquired. "What's her playbook?"

- **Sent engineers to customer sites:** Forced them to see the pain points firsthand. No more coding in a vacuum.

- **Built cross-functional squads:** No more silos. Engineers now work directly with Product & Customer Success.
- **Refocused on performance:** Innovation is great, but only if customers can actually use it.

Bob nodded, impressed. "And how's morale?"

Ava grinned. "Sky-high. They finally trust each other. And for the first time? We're shipping faster than ever. Oh, they ate lots of churros."

Bob leaned back, smiling.

"Sounds like Jane just built her own Dream Team."

RESEARCH—THE FUTURE OF THE COMPANY

Ava circled Research. "This is where Morgan shines."

Bob smirked. "I knew it."

Ava laughed. "Oh, Morgan's not a leader. He's a mad scientist. But put him in the right role? He's unstoppable."

Bob nodded. "What's he working on?"

Ava leaned forward. "Our next-generation AI-driven product."

Bob raised an eyebrow. "Tell me more."

- No setup required. ZERO. AI-driven instant deployment.
- Predictive intelligence. Product adapts to customer needs in real time.
- Industry-first automation. Reduces manual effort by 80%.

Ava grinned. "No more Churro Test. Our next product is going to be instant."

Bob's eyes twinkled, and he stood up as if the meeting was coming to a close.

"We're not done yet," Ava said.

"Oh?" Bob asked and sat again.

WRAPPING UP—THE FINAL PIECE OF THE PUZZLE

Ava picked up the marker one last time and wrote a single word at the top of the whiteboard.

BOARD.

She turned to Bob. "This was the final battle."

Bob leaned back, smiling. "Let me guess—you took no prisoners?"

Ava chuckled. "Oh, I burned the old playbook. I invited the board to dinner the night before our official meeting. Wine was poured, steaks were served, and then I dropped the hammer:

'The board advises. I run the company. Period.'"

Bob raised an eyebrow. "Ballsy."

Ava nodded. "No more telling me what to do. No more telling me who to hire. No more micro-managing my vision. Our board? Brilliant investors. Absolute whizzes with numbers. But let's be real—not a single one of them has actually run a company. They can analyze the hell out of a spreadsheet, but they don't know what it takes to build and scale culture. I had to put them in their place."

Bob smirked. "And how did that go over?"

Ava grinned. "The next day, the board meeting flipped 180 degrees. I brought in my leadership team and let them do the talking. They crushed it. During our closed session, something happened that I never expected—

They stood up and applauded."

Bob's eyes widened. "No way."

Ava laughed, shaking her head. "Yep. I almost cried. And then I told them the truth:

'I am not here to serve the board. I am not here to make investors happy. I am here to build a world-class organization, a culture of excellence, and a business that lasts. If you bet on me just to chase numbers, you bet on the wrong horse.'"

Bob leaned forward, studying her. "And how did you feel at that moment?"

Ava paused. She thought about it. She thought about the journey. The desert. The black boxes. The values she had carved into herself, day by day, decision by decision.

She exhaled. "I felt like I was living AND working my values."

Bob smiled, full of pride.

FINAL THOUGHTS—THE 4-S'S IN ACTION

Bob set down his coffee mug. "Do you know what you've done?"

Ava looked at him, waiting.

Bob pointed at the whiteboard. "You built a company with real balance."

- **You focused on Synergy.** You invested in people, development, and cross-functional teamwork. You hired a strong VP of People, and now you have a sustainable plan to keep your company aligned and thriving.

- **You reignited Spark.** You eliminated the toxicity, tore down silos, and put the right people in the right roles. Your product is finally user-focused and innovative.

- **You didn't lose Strive.** You kept your competitive edge but made sure it wasn't a toxic, cutthroat culture.

- **You restructured without over-indexing on Structure.** You avoided the bureaucratic nightmare that once slowed you down. Now, you have clarity without rigidity.

Bob sat back, arms crossed. "You've built something special, Ava."

She nodded, taking it in.

Bob tapped his temple. "Your company looks more like Apple now. A high-performance, high-innovation culture. Before? You were looking a little too much like Coca-Cola."

Ava laughed. "Yeah, we're not here just to keep the lights on. We're here to change the game."

Bob's eyes flicked to the whiteboard.

Then he noticed something in Ava's expression.

"What's wrong?"

Ava hesitated. Then she sighed. "I lost one more person."

Bob sat up. "Hmmm. Who?"

Ava smiled sadly. "Grace."

Bob's brow furrowed. "Your Chief of Staff?"

Ava nodded. "She was the best partner anyone could ask for. Seven months ago? She literally saved me from myself. She kept the engine running while I was out rediscovering who I was as a leader."

Bob studied her. "So, what happened?"

Ava took a breath. "She outgrew the role. She's too damn smart to be someone's right hand forever. So…"

She grinned.

"…she founded her own startup. And guess what? I'm her first investor."

Bob chuckled. "I bet you are."

Ava teared up, just a little. "I'm so proud of her."

Bob nodded.

"**Good leaders grow other leaders.** That's your social responsibility. If you're doing it right, you'll keep seeing your best people rise and fly. And when that happens? You don't hold them back. You cheer them on."

Ava swallowed hard. "Yeah."

Bob stood up. "And I have a feeling this won't be the last time you watch someone take off."

They both stood there, looking at the whiteboard.

The entire journey laid out in messy, brilliant strokes.

Bob glanced at his watch. "I gotta catch my train. I'm teaching today."

He turned to grab his bag, then paused.

His eyes landed on Ava's desk.

The five artifacts from her journey.

A worn river stone. A delicate teacup. A golden compass.

Bob reached into his pocket and pulled out a small, weathered object.

He placed it on the desk next to Ava's compass.

It was identical.

She looked up at him.

They smiled.

No words needed.

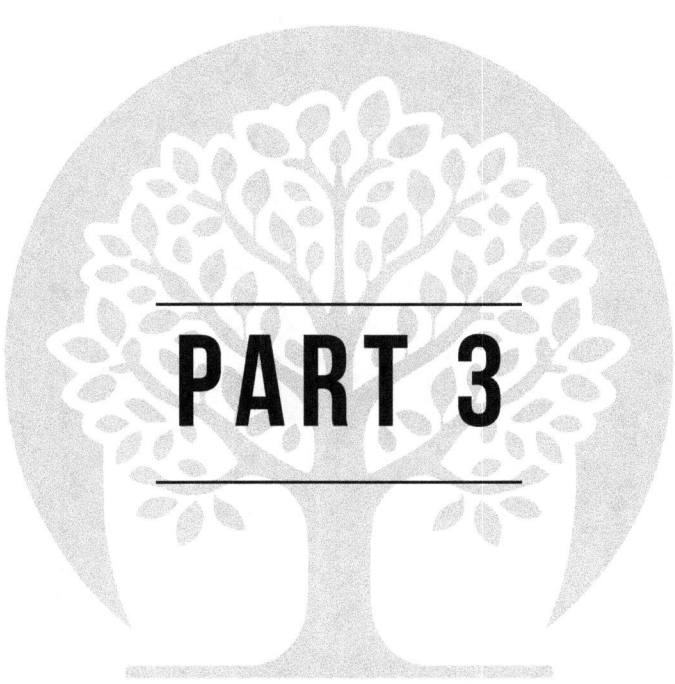

PART 3

THE TOOLS TO MOVE YOU FORWARD

I promised to give you all the tools you need to structure your life and work—and now, you have them.

This book wasn't written to be inspirational fluff that sits on your shelf collecting dust. It's a toolkit. A practical, real-world guide to help you understand, design, and lead a thriving culture—whether at home, in your career, or within an entire organization.

Like any great process, you need a starting point and a roadmap. This is where Part 3 comes in.

TOOLS FOR YOUR JOURNEY

1. **VIBES Assessment:** *Start with YOU.* Take the assessment and see where you land. Before planning out the rest of your journey, you need to know where you stand. Self-awareness is the first step to transformation. Your personal culture defines how you show up in the world—at home, at work, and in life.

2. **4-S Assessment Model:** *Discover Your Organizational Culture.* Think of this as your GPS for organizational success. This tool helps leaders and teams diagnose their current culture ("Now") and define their desired culture ("Preferred"). Organizations that use this effectively create the right foundation for long-term success. If you don't define your culture, it will be defined for you—and usually, not in the way you'd like.

3. **Frequently Asked Questions (FAQs):** Before publishing this book, I had 100 beta readers dig into it, and they asked some fantastic questions. I answered them all, and I'm sharing them with you here. Trust me—there's gold in this section. If you've ever wondered about hiring, leadership, work-life balance, or how to actually apply these tools, you'll find the answers here.

4. **Culture Questions:** *Hire for Values, Not Just Skills.* I have put together powerful interview questions to help you hire people who align with your culture. Every company is different, and culture isn't one-size-fits-all—so take these, adapt them, and make them work for you.

YOUR NEXT STEPS

This isn't just about **reading**—it's about **doing**.

- **Start with VIBES:** Define your personal culture.
- **Use the 4-S Model** to assess and shape your work culture.
- **Apply the FAQs & hiring questions** to build the right team.
- **Commit to deliberate practice:** Culture isn't built in a day.

This book is your playbook. Use it, tweak it, and make it your own.

Culture is intentional. It's the result of thousands of tiny decisions made every single day. The companies that win, the leaders who inspire, and the people who create real impact don't leave culture to chance. They design it, build it, and live it.

Now, it's your turn.

THE VIBES ASSESSMENT

This one is self-explanatory. But here's the catch—you have to be honest with yourself.

If you over-score yourself to stroke your ego or under-score yourself to play it safe, you will stay stuck exactly where you are now. No progress. No change. No transformation. The only way forward is through radical honesty.

Most of this book focused on building your personal culture. I didn't just throw theories at you—I backed everything up with neuroscience, psychology, and lived experience. I gave you exercises, frameworks, and real stories to get your own house in order. Because if you can't master personal culture, you sure as hell won't be able to lead work culture.

Part 3 is where we go deeper into work culture tools—because changing yourself is one thing, but changing an organization? That's a whole different beast.

ORIGINS OF CULTURE—WHERE IT ALL BEGINS

By now, you know that I'm a social scientist and only believe in science and evidence-backed frameworks. I've read hundreds of white papers, thousands of articles and journals, and more books than I can count. And after all of that? My research led me to one undeniable truth about culture.

It all starts at home.

Let me break it down.

Our most formative years are from birth to around 25 years of age. By then, your prefrontal cortex—the part of the brain responsible for decision-making, reasoning, and impulse control—is fully developed. In other words, by 25, your core values are set.

And where do these values come from?

- Parents first
- Friends second
- Teachers third

That's the hierarchy. That's who shapes your worldview. However, you are the CEO of your life and culture. You decide what to learn and practice. You are not going to relive your parents' or friends' or teachers' lives. You are in charge of you.

If you grew up in a home with strong values, psychological safety, and inspiration, you probably had a solid foundation.

If your home culture lacked those things, or worse—if it was full of fear, instability, or emotional neglect, you probably had to unlearn a lot of that as an adult.

That's why breaking toxic cycles is so important. If we don't, we just pass trauma down to the next generation like a family heirloom nobody asked for.

The reality is childhood trauma is the leading cause of anxiety in our culture. And if you don't process it, you will pass it on—whether you mean to or not.

But here's the good news: you can stop the cycle.

You can say, "F**k that. I'm going to be different."

You can choose to be the first in your family to break the loop.

WHAT THIS MEANS FOR LEADERSHIP

If personal culture comes from home, what does that mean for work culture?

Simple. The best leaders create environments that feel safe, stable, and inspiring—just like the best parents.

Companies don't need more ego-driven bosses barking orders and micromanaging people into oblivion.

They need leaders who create trust, clarity, and purpose.

I was lucky enough to figure this out through years of trial, error, and failure. And as a parent, my wife and I made the decision to be intentional about raising good, kind humans who could one day become inspirational leaders.

Because let's be real—we need more of those.

THE VIBES ASSESSMENT – DISCOVER YOUR STRENGTHS & AREAS FOR GROWTH

Use this assessment to evaluate how well you embody the **VIBES** framework in your personal and professional life. Rate yourself on a scale of 1 (low) to 5 (high) for each question.

V – Values & Beliefs (Your Inner Compass)

How well do your values guide your decisions and actions?

1. I have a clear understanding of my core values and can articulate them easily.

   1   2   3   4   5

2. When faced with a tough decision, I refer to my values to guide my choice.

   1   2   3   4   5

3. My daily actions reflect what I believe is important in life and work.

   1   2   3   4   5

4. I set boundaries that align with my values, even when it's uncomfortable.

1   2   3   4   5

5. I feel confident that my personal and professional life are in alignment with my values.

1   2   3   4   5

I – Interaction & Communication (The Language of Connection)

How well do you connect with others through listening and communication?

1. I actively listen in conversations, focusing on understanding rather than just responding.

1   2   3   4   5

2. I ask thoughtful questions to deepen my relationships and professional connections.

1   2   3   4   5

3. I handle conflicts with a calm and constructive approach rather than reacting emotionally.

1   2   3   4   5

4. I am aware of my nonverbal communication (tone, facial expressions, body language).

1   2   3   4   5

5. I create a culture of open and honest communication in my personal or professional life.

1   2   3   4   5

B – Behaviors & Rituals (The Power of Small Actions)

How consistent are you in maintaining habits and rituals that support your goals?

1. I have daily or weekly routines that help me stay productive and balanced.

   1   2   3   4   5

2. I follow through on commitments and avoid procrastination.

   1   2   3   4   5

3. I celebrate small wins and recognize progress, not just big achievements.

   1   2   3   4   5

4. I have set rituals (morning, work, or evening) that help me stay grounded.

   1   2   3   4   5

5. I understand that consistent effort, rather than bursts of motivation, leads to long-term success.

   1   2   3   4   5

E – Environment & Space (Designing for Success)

How well does your environment support your focus and well-being?

1. My workspace (whether at home or in an office) is organized and distraction-free.

| 1 | 2 | 3 | 4 | 5 |

2. I intentionally create an environment that enhances my productivity and creativity.

| 1 | 2 | 3 | 4 | 5 |

3. I take breaks and manage screen time to maintain focus and avoid burnout.

| 1 | 2 | 3 | 4 | 5 |

4. I pay attention to the lighting, sounds, and setup of my workspace to improve my energy.

| 1 | 2 | 3 | 4 | 5 |

5. I have a clear separation between work and personal life, even when working remotely.

| 1 | 2 | 3 | 4 | 5 |

S – SUPPORT & LEADERSHIP (THE STRENGTH OF COMMUNITY)

How well do you build trust, collaborate, and support others?

1. I have mentors, advisors, or trusted voices who challenge and support me.

| 1 | 2 | 3 | 4 | 5 |

2. I offer guidance, encouragement, or mentorship to others in my community or workplace.

| 1 | 2 | 3 | 4 | 5 |

3. I trust my team or colleagues and empower them rather than micromanaging.

1	2	3	4	5

4. I feel comfortable asking for help or feedback when needed.

1	2	3	4	5

5. I create or contribute to a positive and supportive culture in my work and personal life.

1	2	3	4	5

Scoring & Reflection

Total your scores for each section:

- V (Values & Beliefs): _____ / 25
- I (Interaction & Communication): _____ / 25
- B (Behaviors & Rituals): _____ / 25
- E (Environment & Space): _____ / 25
- S (Support & Leadership): _____ / 25

What Your Score Means

- **21-25:** This is a strength for you! Keep reinforcing these habits.
- **16-20:** You're doing well, but there's room for refinement.
- **11-15:** Some areas need attention—small changes will have a big impact.
- **5-10:** This is a growth area—consider focusing on this aspect to improve your overall success and fulfillment.

NEXT STEPS

1. Identify the area where you scored the lowest.

2. Choose one small habit or action from the VIBES framework to improve.

3. Set a 30-day challenge to implement a new habit, such as:

   - Clarifying your values.
   - Practicing active listening.
   - Creating a focused life and work environment.
   - Establishing daily rituals.
   - Building a stronger support network.

THE 4-S ASSESSMENT

I built the 4-S model after years of testing, failing, refining, and testing again. If you've studied organizational development, like I did, you'll see some familiar concepts. But let's be real – some of that stuff is just over-thought and over-complicated because it was cooked up by theorists. I took the best of what I learned, combined it with real-world, tested experience, and built a modern, straightforward, no-BS version that anyone can use.

And here's the best part: it's free to you. Use the login details provided in this book and get to work.

If you find the ideas, tools, and assessments useful, do me one favor—tell a friend.

I didn't write this book to build my ego. I didn't write it to sell workshops (even though it's a good way to spread the word), slap my name on some overpriced corporate training, or convince you that I have all the answers. I want to start a revolution, so could you!

I want you, your teams, your companies, your communities—hell, even your families—to have the right tools to build a value-driven culture.

This book doesn't belong on a shelf collecting dust. It belongs in your hands, in your conversations, in your work, in your life.

Culture is what we do every day.

So go do it.

THE 4-S ASSESSMENT: DISCOVER YOUR ORGANIZATIONAL CULTURE

Culture is often treated like some mystical, intangible force. Something you just "feel" but can't quite measure. Well, that's bullshit.

The 4-S Model exists to cut through the noise and give leaders hard data on what's really happening inside their organizations. No fluff. No guessing. No "gut feelings." Just measurable, actionable insights that separate great companies from the ones stuck in dysfunction.

This isn't just an assessment; it's a diagnostic tool—like an MRI for your company's culture. If you want to build a culture of excellence, the first step is understanding where you actually are today.

HOW THE 4-S MODEL WORKS

At its core, **the 4-S Model** measures where your organization stands across four key dimensions:

- **Synergy:** Do your teams collaborate? Do people feel connected?
- **Spark:** Is your company innovative? Do you embrace change?
- **Strive:** Is your company competitive? Are you pushing for market leadership?
- **Structure:** Do you have strong processes? Is there clarity and stability?

Now, let's break down how it works.

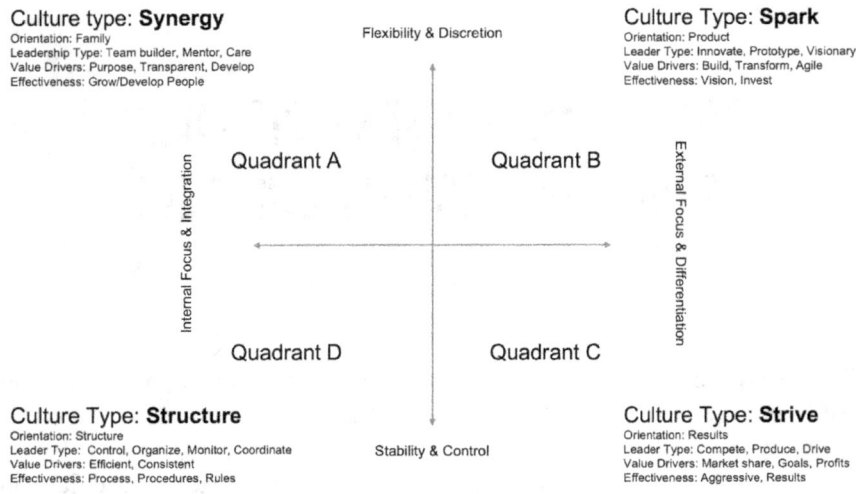

Illustration 5

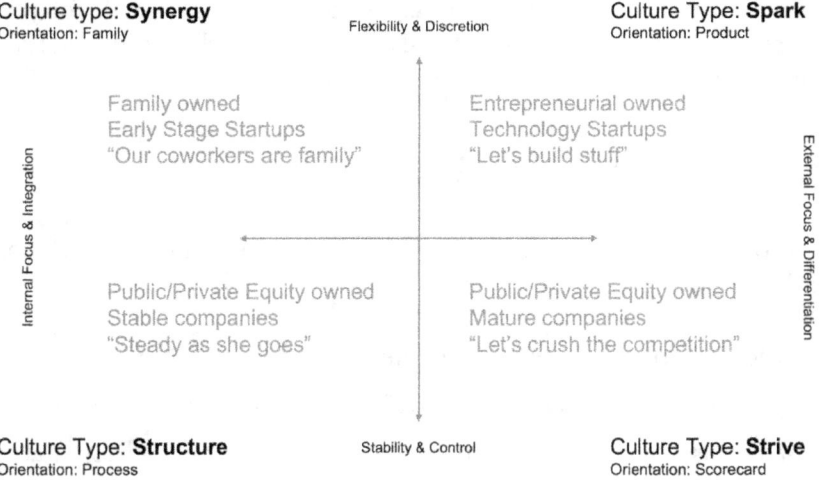

Illustration 6

THE TWO AXES OF CULTURE

Think of the 4-S framework like a map with two intersecting axes:

- **Vertical Axis:** Flexibility & Discretion at the top vs. Stability & Control at the bottom.
- **Horizontal Axis:** Internal Focus & Integration on the left vs. External Focus & Differentiation on the right.

Each quadrant reflects a distinct culture type based on how flexible, structured, internally, or externally focused the company is.

WHAT THE 4-S ASSESSMENT MEASURES

Each quadrant is broken down into four critical dimensions:

1. **Orientation:** What's the company's natural tendency?

2. **Leadership Style:** How do leaders behave?

3. **Value Drivers:** What motivates people to perform?

4. **Effectiveness:** What actually works?

This takes less than five minutes to complete. But—just like the VIBES assessment—radical honesty is key. If you game the answers, you're only lying to yourself.

STEP 1: RUNNING THE CULTURAL DIAGNOSTICS

There's an old Chinese proverb that says:

> *"A journey of a thousand miles begins with a single step."*

In business, that first step is understanding your current culture.

Too many leaders assume they know their culture—but assumptions are dangerous. Some CEOs think, "Oh, we have a great culture," while their employees are quite quitting en masse. Others believe "We're all about innovation," while their teams feel stifled by endless bureaucracy.

The reality?

There's often a massive gap between how leaders perceive their culture and what's actually happening on the ground.

That's why you need real data. And not cherry-picked feedback from the loudest voices in the room.

Who Should Take the 4-S?

The more participants, the better.

At a minimum, these groups should take the assessment:

- Leadership Team – Since leaders set the culture, their alignment is critical.
- Managers & Extended Leadership – To identify gaps between leadership and execution.
- **Departments & Teams:** To spot subcultures and disconnects across functions.

The 4-S can generate reports at multiple levels:

- **Company-Wide Report:** The big picture.
- **Leadership Report:** How aligned are the execs?
- **Department Reports:** Are there cultural divides?
- **Team Reports:** Which managers are shaping (or breaking) culture?
- **Individual Reports:** Why do some employees struggle to "fit in"?

Each of these cuts of the data provides a clearer picture of where cultural gaps exist.

Common Cultural Misalignments

Every company has two dominant culture types that define them. But here's where things get interesting.

Some teams naturally skew toward certain quadrants:

- Sales teams lean toward Strive (competitive, numbers-driven).
- Product & R&D lean toward Spark (innovation-focused).
- Customer Success & HR lean toward Synergy (people-oriented).
- Finance & Operations lean toward Structure (process-heavy).

But what happens when one department completely misaligns with the company's overall culture?

Warning Signs of Cultural Dysfunction

- The CEO's perception is wildly different from employees.
- One department is operating in a completely different quadrant than the rest of the company.
- Certain managers are fostering subcultures that conflict with company values.
- Employees feel disconnected, disengaged, or misaligned.

Ignoring these red flags is a recipe for disaster.

The goal? Identify where cultural breakdowns exist—before they turn into full-blown crises.

STEP 2: INTERPRETING YOUR 4-S RESULTS

Once you've run the assessment, the next step is understanding what it all means.

You'll get two key data points:

- **NOW Culture:** Where you currently are.
- **PREFERRED Culture:** Where people want to be.

The bigger the gap between NOW and PREFERRED, the more work you have to do.

How to Use the Results

If your entire company is leaning toward Structure but your leadership team thinks you're all about Spark, that's a disconnect.

If your sales department is deep in Strive, but your product team is pure Synergy, you might be dealing with internal friction that's slowing down execution.

Interpreting the data isn't about judgment. It's about understanding where you are so you can take deliberate action.

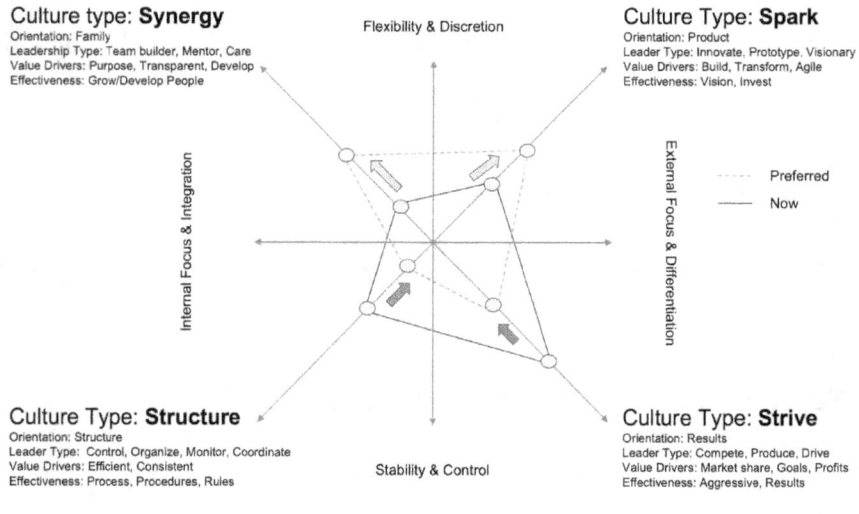

Culture type: Synergy
Orientation: Family
Leadership Type: Team builder, Mentor, Care
Value Drivers: Purpose, Transparent, Develop
Effectiveness: Grow/Develop People

Flexibility & Discretion

Culture Type: Spark
Orientation: Product
Leader Type: Innovate, Prototype, Visionary
Value Drivers: Build, Transform, Agile
Effectiveness: Vision, Invest

Internal Focus & Integration

External Focus & Differentiation

- - - - - Preferred
———— Now

Culture Type: Structure
Orientation: Structure
Leader Type: Control, Organize, Monitor, Coordinate
Value Drivers: Efficient, Consistent
Effectiveness: Process, Procedures, Rules

Stability & Control

Culture Type: Strive
Orientation: Results
Leader Type: Compete, Produce, Drive
Value Drivers: Market share, Goals, Profits
Effectiveness: Aggressive, Results

Illustration 7

The Power of Real Data

There's a reason the best companies in the world invest in culture.

MIT Sloan found that companies with strong cultures see 4x higher revenue growth. Harvard Business Review reported that culture-driven organizations outperform competitors by 200%. Gallup's research shows that engaged employees are 21% more productive.

The 4-S isn't just a feel-good exercise. It's a science-backed framework designed to help you run a better company.

If you're serious about culture, this is the foundation.

So go take the assessment. Be honest. Get your data. And then?

Get to work.

Sample Culture Types listed on illustrations 8-14 (see below).

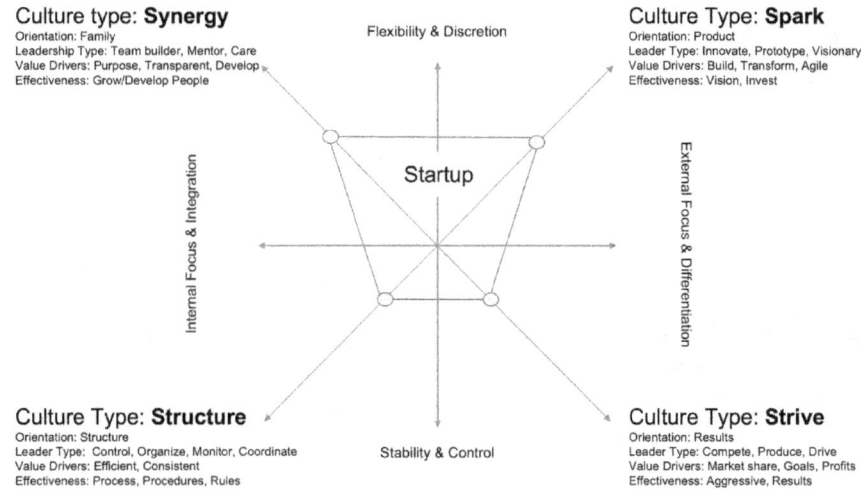

Illustration 8

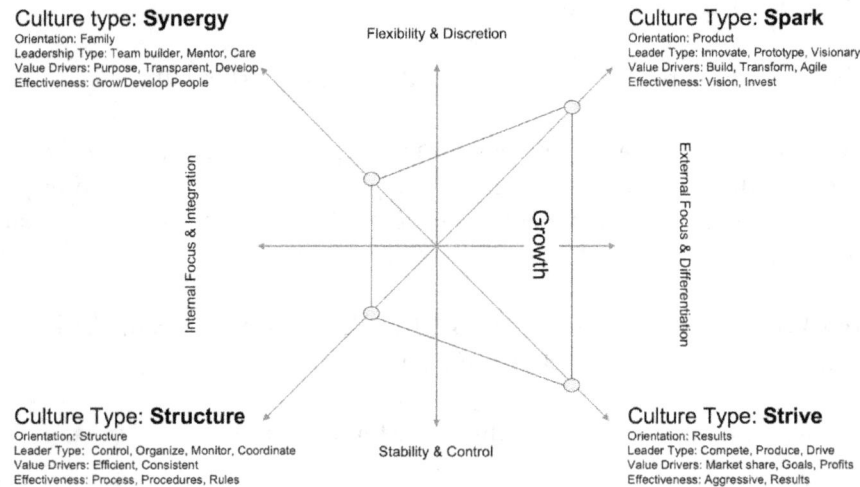

Illustration 9

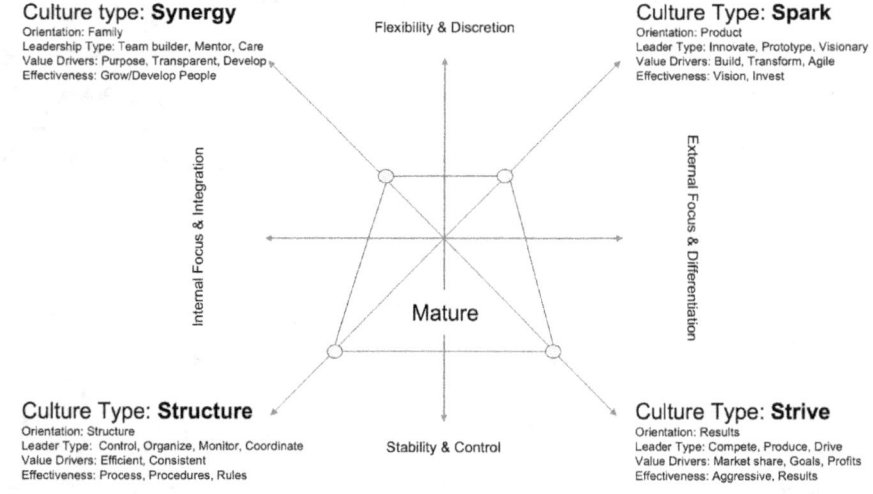

Illustration 10

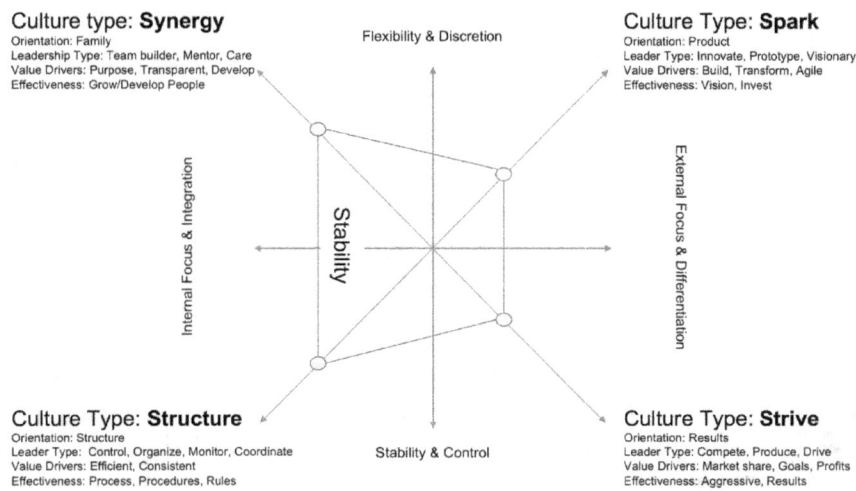

Illustration 11

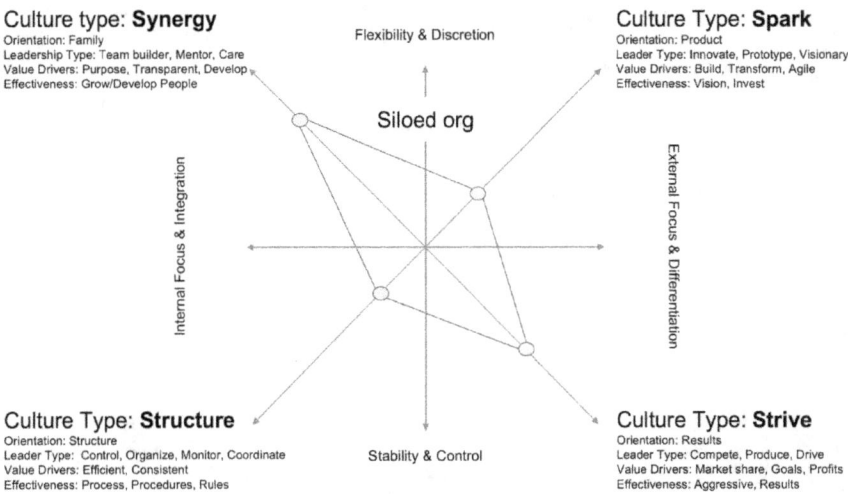

Illustration 12

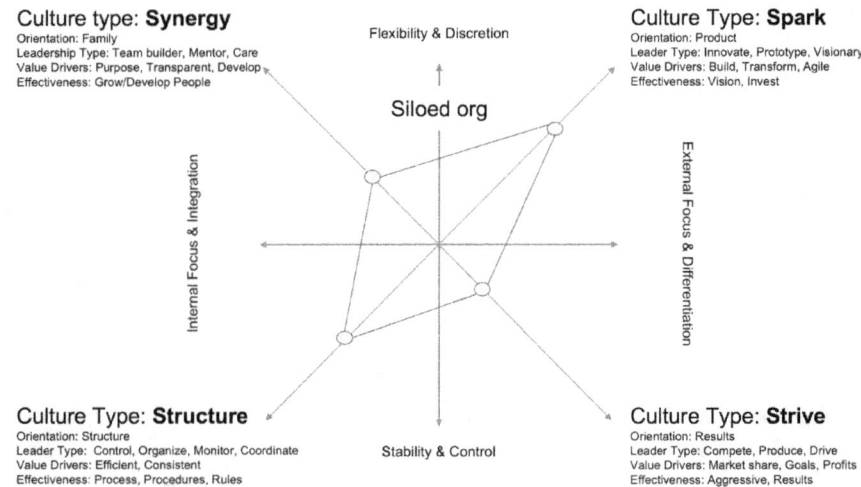

Illustration 13

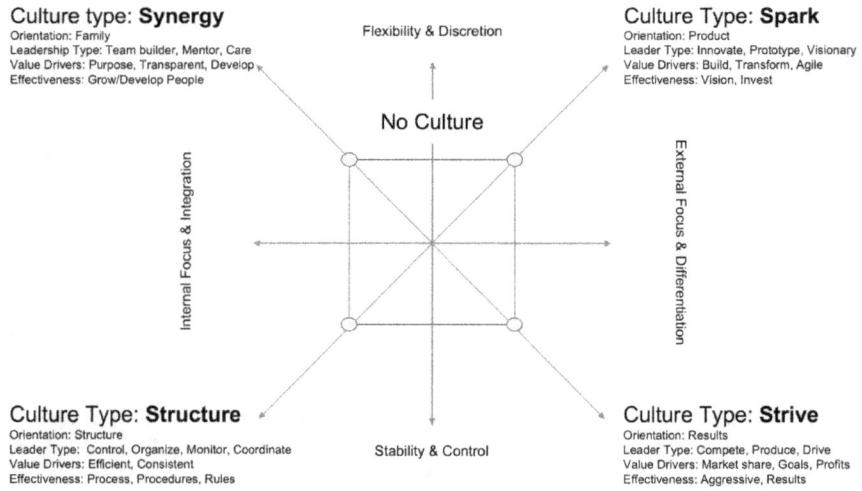

Illustration 14

STEP 3: BUILDING THE ACTION PLAN

You have the data. You've interpreted the results. Now comes the hard part: actually doing something about it.

Culture isn't a one-and-done project. It's a living, breathing organism. Even the best organizations constantly nurture it, refine it, and evolve. If you're not actively shaping your culture, entropy will do it for you. And trust me—you won't like what grows in an untended garden.

Every organization falls into one of five cultural scenarios. Your 4-S results will tell you where you stand.

Where Does Your Company Fall?

Scenario 1: Excellence in Action

The company has a strong culture of excellence. People love working here. Low attrition, high engagement, strong values. Culture is an asset, not a liability.

> WHAT TO DO: *Stay vigilant. Even great cultures can slip. Evolve without losing what makes you great. Keep reinforcing behaviors that made you successful.*
>
> REAL-WORLD EXAMPLE: *Apple in the early 2000s. They had a relentless focus on innovation, strong leadership, and a mission-driven culture. But they never got complacent—they kept raising the bar.*

Scenario 2: Fine-Tune

The company is doing well but slightly off-track. Some teams are fully aligned, others are drifting. Employees feel engaged but see room for improvement.

WHAT TO DO: *Identify small areas of misalignment and course correct. Fine-tune leadership behaviors and team dynamics. Increase transparency and communication.*

REAL-WORLD EXAMPLE: *Netflix in the 2010s. They had a strong culture of freedom and responsibility, but when they scaled, some of that transparency started to break down. They adjusted policies without losing their core DNA.*

Scenario 3: Needs Some Work

The company is off-track, and employees know it. Engagement scores are dipping. People are frustrated. Some values are being lived, others ignored.

WHAT TO DO: *Reinforce company values—through actions, not words. Rebuild trust between leadership and employees. Identify and fix systemic cultural issues (lack of feedback, poor leadership behaviors, weak accountability).*

REAL-WORLD EXAMPLE: *Microsoft pre-Satya Nadella. Before Nadella took over, Microsoft had a toxic, overly competitive internal culture. He reset the company's values—shifting from control and bureaucracy to learning and collaboration.*

Scenario 4: Transformation Intervention

The culture is broken. Employees are disengaged or leaving. Toxic leadership, bureaucracy, or outdated processes are killing innovation. Misalignment between what leadership says and what employees experience.

WHAT TO DO: *Hit the reset button on leadership accountability. Remove toxic leaders. Culture killers have to go. Rebuild trust through transparency, consistency, and action.*

REAL-WORLD EXAMPLE: *Uber under Travis Kalanick. Their culture was cutthroat, toxic, and unsustainable. After an internal crisis, the company restructured leadership, refocused on integrity, and rebuilt its values.*

Scenario 5: Starting Out

The company is new and building culture from scratch. Values aren't yet defined, but leadership has an opportunity to be intentional. A great culture is possible—if built deliberately.

> **WHAT TO DO:** *Codify your values early. Don't let culture "just happen." Hire people who match the culture you want to create. Build leadership behaviors that reinforce the right principles from day one.*
>
> **REAL-WORLD EXAMPLE:** *Stripe in its early days. The founders built a deeply intentional, thoughtful culture from the start—focusing on long-term thinking, customer obsession, and high performance.*

The CEO Owns Culture—Period.

If you're the CEO, culture is your #1 job. If you're a leader, you co-own it with your team. If you have a People/HR team, they enable it—but they don't own it.

Here's where most organizations screw up:

- They outsource culture to HR.
- They think culture is "soft" and don't measure it.
- They focus on perks instead of behaviors.

A People team is essential—but they're not responsible for fixing culture. Leadership is. If the CEO and leadership team aren't fully committed to cultural transformation, it will never happen.

What's Next?

Once you know your current culture, the next step is building the roadmap to get to your ideal state.

Step 4 is all about execution. You've done the diagnostics; you've created the plan—now it's time to put it into action.

This is where real leaders separate themselves from the rest.

So, ask yourself: **Are you going to let culture "happen" to your company? Or are you going to take control and build something great?**

The answer to that question will define your legacy.

Now, let's move to Step 4: Executing the Culture Plan.

STEP 4: EXECUTING THE CULTURE PLAN

You've gathered the data, interpreted the results, and set a plan—now comes the hard part: making it real.

Most culture initiatives fail at execution because leaders: Treat it like a one-time event instead of an ongoing discipline. Think sending a company-wide email is enough. Fail to hold themselves and others accountable.

Culture is not a poster on the wall, a mission statement, or a catchy set of values. It's what people do every day when no one is watching.

Now, let's talk about how to make culture stick.

The Culture Execution Playbook

There are **five key levers** to ensure that culture transformation actually happens:

Leadership Behavior—Setting the Tone from the Top

Leaders don't just talk about culture. They model it. What leaders tolerate, they endorse. Employees watch what leaders do more than what they say.

> **EXECUTION PLAN:** *Set a "Culture Contract" with your leadership team— what behaviors will you commit to? Hold monthly leadership alignment*

> *meetings to reinforce expectations. Catch leaders when they slip—peer accountability is key.*
>
> **CASE STUDY:** *Microsoft under Satya Nadella—Nadella flipped Microsoft's rigid, top-down culture by personally modeling a "learn-it-all" mindset. Instead of punishing failure, he encouraged curiosity and innovation. Employees followed his lead.*

Systems & Processes—Embedding Culture in Everyday Work

Culture isn't just "vibes." It's reinforced by how work gets done. Your hiring, performance management, and rewards systems must align with your culture. If your systems contradict your culture, people will follow the system—not your values.

> **EXECUTION PLAN:** *Hire for ABC (Abilities, Behaviors, Culture fit)—every hire either strengthens or weakens culture. Replace "Performance Reviews" with Growth Reviews—measure learning, not just output. Reward behaviors that reinforce culture—public recognition, bonuses, career growth.*
>
> **CASE STUDY:** *Netflix & the "Keeper Test" — Netflix's famous performance philosophy asks managers: "If this person were leaving for another company, would you fight to keep them?" If the answer is not a clear yes, they let them go. It's brutal—but it ensures only the best cultural fits stay.*

Communication—Creating a Shared Language

A strong culture has a strong internal language. Words shape behavior—people need shorthand to reinforce the right actions. Without constant storytelling, values become just words on a website.

> **EXECUTION PLAN:** *Start every meeting with a Culture Story—how someone lived the company's values. Use consistent phrases—Google's "psychological safety" or Amazon's "disagree and commit." Make culture part of your leadership Q&As, town halls, and Slack channels.*

> **CASE STUDY:** *Amazon's "Day One" Mentality—Jeff Bezos constantly reinforced that Amazon should operate like a startup, even at scale. By making "Day One" part of the company's language, employees understood they should always move fast, innovate, and avoid bureaucracy.*

Reinforcement—Holding People Accountable

Culture isn't what you preach—it's what you enforce. Bad behavior must have consequences, no matter how talented the person is. Toxic high-performers destroy culture faster than low-performers.

> **EXECUTION PLAN:** *Fire culture-killers fast—don't let them linger. Call out bad behavior in real-time—silence = approval. Make cultural fit a hard requirement for promotions and raises.*
>
> **CASE STUDY:** *Airbnb's "Culture Interview" — Every new hire at Airbnb had to pass a culture interview—completely separate from technical skills. Even if they were an A+ engineer, if they weren't a fit for Airbnb's culture, they didn't get hired.*

Culture is a Marathon, Not a Sprint

Culture isn't a one-time project. It's a continuous cycle of:

1. Assessing reality (4-S Assessment)

2. Interpreting the data (Where are we now?)

3. Planning the changes (What's the action plan?)

4. Executing relentlessly (Making it real every single day)

The best companies never stop working on culture.

If you want to build a culture of excellence, you can't "set it and forget it."

So, ask yourself:

Are you going to lead your culture—or let it lead you?

Your move.

STEP 5: MEASURING CULTURE—TRACKING PROGRESS & STAYING HONEST

You can't manage what you don't measure. Culture isn't "fluffy"—it should have clear, trackable metrics. Without measurement, culture will always take a backseat to "urgent" business needs.

Leaders who don't track culture metrics tend to assume everything is fine—until it isn't. By the time they realize there's a problem, turnover is high, morale is low, and customers are feeling the ripple effects. The best leaders don't wait for culture to crash—they monitor it like they monitor revenue.

How to Measure Culture Like a Pro

There are **four key metrics** that separate great cultures from dysfunctional ones:

4-S Culture Assessment—Benchmark & Track Progress

If you don't take a baseline measurement, how will you know if you're improving? The 4-S Culture Assessment should be taken every six months to track shifts in culture over time.

> **EXECUTION PLAN:** *Have every employee take the 4-S Assessment. Compare NOW vs. PREFERRED scores—where's the biggest gap? Track cultural trends—are you moving toward or away from your ideal culture?*
>
> **CASE STUDY:** *Microsoft's Cultural Shift — When Satya Nadella took over as CEO, he didn't just make sweeping leadership changes—he measured cultural transformation. By tracking employee engagement and cultural alignment, he proved that culture changes could be tracked just like financial metrics.*

Employee Net Promoter Score (eNPS)—Would Your Employees Recommend Working Here?

eNPS = % of Promoters – % of Detractors

Score range: -100 to +100 (higher is better)
Great cultures score above +50

The most honest feedback about culture comes from employees who've been through it. Would they recommend working at your company to their best friend? If not, you have a problem.

> **EXECUTION PLAN:** *Run eNPS surveys every six months. Identify why detractors are unhappy and fix those issues. Celebrate what promoters love and reinforce it.*

> **CASE STUDY:** *Google's "Project Oxygen" — Google ran deep-dive employee surveys to find out what made a great manager. They discovered that psychological safety was the #1 predictor of high-performing teams—so they started measuring it in leadership assessments.*

Attrition & Hiring Trends—Who's Leaving & Why?

- **Voluntary turnover:** Are your best people leaving?
- **Involuntary turnover:** Are you firing culture misfits fast enough?
- **Hiring trends:** Are new hires staying past 12 months?

High turnover isn't always bad—losing toxic employees can improve culture. But if your best people are leaving, it's a sign of cultural decay.

> **EXECUTION PLAN:** *Exit interviews – Track why people leave. New hire retention – If 30% of new hires quit in six months, your hiring process is broken. Leader turnover – If you're losing top leaders, culture might be the root cause.*

> **CASE STUDY:** *Netflix's Culture Purge — When Reed Hastings overhauled Netflix's culture, he made one thing clear: no brilliant jerks allowed. The*

> *result? High turnover in year one—but a stronger, more aligned culture moving forward.*

Performance & Engagement Scores—Are People Thriving?

High engagement = higher productivity, retention & innovation. Low engagement = quiet quitting, resentment & burnout. Engagement drives business results—companies with highly engaged teams outperform their peers by 21% (Gallup).

- **Execution Plan:** Run engagement surveys quarterly—track trends over time.
- **Measure manager effectiveness:** bad managers kill engagement fast.
- **Tie engagement to business KPIs:** if engagement drops, expect revenue to follow.

> **CASE STUDY:** *Salesforce's "Ohana Culture" Metrics — Salesforce continuously tracks employee engagement, leadership effectiveness, and culture alignment. If scores dip, leadership intervenes before problems spiral.*

Culture is Everything and Everywhere

Culture isn't just something that exists in the workplace—it's woven into the fabric of our daily lives. It's in our homes, our schools, our communities, our hobbies, our sports teams, our social media interactions, and even the way we gather for dinner. Whether you realize it or not, **culture is shaping you every single day.**

Culture in Everyday Life

Culture isn't just a workplace phenomenon—it's everywhere. It's the invisible force that shapes our decisions, our behaviors, and the way we connect with others.

At Home. The way a family operates is its own culture. Some families have structured routines and formal dinner conversations, while others thrive in chaos and spontaneity. Some parents value independence, while others emphasize collectivism. The way we were raised becomes the foundation of how we see the world.

In Schools. Walk into any school, and you'll immediately feel its culture. Some schools prioritize academic excellence, while others emphasize creativity and social-emotional learning. Some have a culture of competition, while others focus on inclusivity. Teachers and administrators set the tone—just like leaders in a company.

In Sports. Every sports team has a culture. The New England Patriots built a dynasty on discipline and "The Patriot Way." The Golden State Warriors created a culture of unselfishness and ball movement. Internationally, soccer powerhouses like Brazil thrive on flair and individual skill, while Germany dominates through precision and discipline. Same game, different cultures.

In Hobbies & Social Groups. Whether it's a local book club, a cycling team, a gaming community, or community theater, every group forms its own culture. Some prioritize competition, others are purely social. Look around at any group you're a part of—the unwritten rules and values create its culture.

On social media: Every platform has a distinct culture.

- LinkedIn is professional and curated.
- Twitter (X) is snarky and fast-paced.
- Instagram is visual storytelling.
- TikTok is raw, unfiltered creativity.
- Facebook is like your family group chat—nostalgic, opinionated, and still sharing memes from 2012.

The way people interact on each platform is shaped by the culture of that digital space. Even online, culture is alive.

In Music: Music is one of the most powerful cultural forces in the world. Every genre has a different culture—Hip-hop was born from resilience and storytelling, Jazz thrives on improvisation and freedom, Rock is rebellion and energy, Classical is discipline and tradition. Even within electronic music, House culture is about community and inclusivity, while Techno is about raw energy and underground movements. Music doesn't just entertain—it carries values, emotions, and entire cultural movements.

Culture isn't one thing—it's everything. It's the heartbeat of our families, our schools, our teams, our hobbies, our digital spaces, and the music we listen to.

And the best part? Culture can change. It all depends on the people brave enough to shape it.

Culture isn't one thing—it's everything

Culture: A Living, Breathing Organism

Culture isn't static. It's not a framed mission statement hanging on a wall or a list of values buried in an onboarding deck. Culture is alive—it evolves, it reacts, it thrives, or it withers.

And just like a living organism, it needs three things to survive: nutrition, rest, and movement.

1. Nutrition: What You Feed It, It Becomes

A body fed with junk deteriorates. A culture fed with negativity, fear, and inconsistency? Same outcome. On the other hand, when you fuel an organization with trust, purpose, and shared values, it flourishes.

Think of your workplace (or home, or social circle) like a garden. You can't plant seeds and walk away expecting a thriving ecosystem. You have to nurture it—pull out the weeds (toxic behaviors), water the roots (reinforce core values), and expose it to sunlight (transparency and communication). If you neglect it, weeds take over, and the wrong things start growing.

> **REAL-WORLD LESSON:** *Ever been in a company where bad behavior is tolerated because "he's a top performer" or "that's just how things are here"? That's the equivalent of letting one rotten fruit spoil the whole basket. Ignore it long enough, and the whole culture starts to stink.*

2. Rest: Recovery Builds Strength

Just like athletes need recovery days, culture needs time to breathe and reset. An organization that's all hustle, grind, and "always-on" eventually burns out—both its people and its values.

The problem? We've been trained to think of *work-life balance* as squeezing in personal time around work. That's outdated. It's time to flip it: life comes first, then work supports it.

Companies that understand this shift—from *work-life* to life-work—build cultures that sustain performance *without* burning people out. They recognize that employees who are rested, fulfilled, and have time for personal growth actually perform better and stick around longer.

> **REAL-WORLD LESSON:** *Think of the last time you took a real break. Not a "pretend vacation" where you secretly checked emails. A full disconnect. When you came back, weren't you sharper? More creative? More engaged? That's because our best work doesn't come from exhaustion—it comes from recovery.*

The best leaders don't glorify burnout; they prioritize rest as part of the success formula. They create space for teams to recharge, reflect, and reset—which ironically leads to higher productivity, not lower.

> **CULTURE CHECK:** *Does your workplace celebrate overwork like a badge of honor? Does your manager send you a Friday night email and start a fire-drill that makes you work all weekend? If so, you're on a path to burnout, not brilliance. The best organizations actively fight against burnout by shifting from work-life to life-work.*
>
> **SIMPLE FIX:** *Normalize real breaks. Whether it's no-meeting Fridays, built-in recovery weeks, or a culture where unplugging is actually encouraged (not just lip service), giving people space to recharge is a competitive advantage.*

Because in the long run? The well-rested outperform the overworked.

3. Movement: Adapt or Die

Organisms that don't move? They stagnate. Cultures that don't adapt? They die. The best organizations aren't the ones that *have* culture—they're the ones that actively build and rebuild it.

Companies like Netflix and Apple have reinvented themselves multiple times, and their cultures evolved alongside them. The ones that refused to move became cautionary tales.

> **REAL-WORLD LESSON:** *Remember that company that had an amazing culture … until it scaled? Suddenly, what used to be a collaborative, transparent environment turned into bureaucratic chaos with meetings about meetings. Culture needs constant recalibration—what worked at 50 employees won't work at 500.*

Culture is the Spirit of Humanity

If nutrition, rest, and movement keep culture *alive*, then spirit is what makes it human.

Culture isn't just an organizational thing—it's deeply personal. It's the collective energy of the people who shape it. That's why the same company with the same policies can feel radically different depending on the leadership.

Have you ever walked into a company where you instantly felt the energy? Some places buzz with excitement, others feel like you just stepped into a corporate graveyard. That's spirit.

> **REAL-WORLD LESSON:** *Ever been part of a team where, despite the long hours and stress, you felt unstoppable because you actually cared about what you were building together? That's culture at its best—it connects people to something bigger than themselves.*

Culture is Your Personality (and Your Organization's Personality)

If culture had a dating profile, what would be the vibe it gives off?

- Is it welcoming or intimidating?
- Does it have a sense of humor, or is it strictly business?
- Does it uplift people or burn them out?

Just like individuals have personalities, organizations have them too. And guess what? Just like people, organizations attract others who match their energy.

> **REAL-WORLD LESSON:** *Have you ever joined a company where you felt like a total outsider, no matter how qualified you were? Like you spoke a completely different language than everyone else? That's a culture mismatch. It's not you, it's them. (Or maybe it's you, but that's another conversation.)*

What Culture Are You Building?

Culture isn't something you "set and forget." It's alive, it's human, it's evolving. The question is:

Are you intentionally shaping it, or are you letting it shape itself?

Because just like an untended garden, a culture left on autopilot doesn't grow the way you want it to.

Culture Around the World

Ava's journey wasn't just about escaping the chaos of work—it was a global case study on culture. She traveled to five different parts of the world to prove one thing: Culture is different, but the framework we outlined is universal.

Values are values, no matter where you go. Culture is shaped by leaders—whether that's a CEO, a head coach, a teacher, or a parent. Great cultures don't happen by accident—they are built with intention.

Let's take a quick trip around the world:

Japan: A culture built on respect, harmony, and precision. The Japanese concept of "Kaizen" (continuous improvement) is embedded in their workplaces, homes, and even their approach to craftsmanship. Whether it's making sushi, designing technology, or playing baseball, they focus on mastery and discipline.

Brazil: A culture of joy, passion, and spontaneity. From carnival celebrations to the way they play soccer, Brazilians embrace energy and creativity. Their culture thrives on relationships and personal connections—business deals are built on trust, not just contracts.

Germany: A culture of structure, efficiency, and precision. Whether it's their engineering, work ethic, or even their punctuality, Germans take pride in order and reliability. The Strive & Structure quadrants of the 4-S model are dominant in German workplaces.

South Africa: A culture of resilience and unity. The concept of "Ubuntu" (I am because we are) shapes their society, emphasizing interconnectedness and community. After decades of apartheid, South Africa built a culture centered on reconciliation and togetherness.

India: A culture of innovation and adaptability. From the tech industry to Bollywood, India's ability to blend tradition with rapid modernization makes it a fascinating case study in how cultures evolve over time.

Same world, different cultures—but the framework of values, leadership, and team dynamics is universal.

Culture is Spiritual

Beyond the workplace, beyond communities, beyond countries—culture is deeply spiritual.

For thousands of years, human beings have passed down stories that define who we are. From ancient religious texts to modern-day fables, the stories we tell shape the cultures we live in.

Every religious and spiritual tradition has its own guiding principles, but at their core, they all share one thing: a belief in something greater than ourselves.

In Christianity, the Bible tells stories of faith, resilience, and redemption. From Moses leading people to freedom to Jesus teaching love and forgiveness, the lessons have shaped cultures worldwide.

In Buddhism, the teachings of the Buddha emphasize inner peace, wisdom, and the path to enlightenment. Entire societies have been built on these principles, fostering cultures of mindfulness and balance.

In Islam, the Quran provides guidance on how to live a just and moral life. The emphasis on community and discipline has influenced countless nations and their cultural foundations.

In Hinduism, the Bhagavad Gita teaches duty, purpose, and the eternal struggle between right and wrong. Its lessons transcend time, guiding generations on how to navigate life's challenges.

In Indigenous traditions, oral storytelling is sacred—passed down through generations to preserve wisdom, honor ancestors, and connect with nature.

The **human spirit is what drives us to tell stories**—to teach lessons, to choose good over bad, to live fulfilled lives. Culture and spirituality are intertwined, shaping how we treat one another and how we build the world around us.

Your Story, Your Culture

This was Ava's story.

But in reality? It was a collection of stories.

Stories I picked up throughout my personal and professional life. Stories of failures and breakthroughs. Stories of people who inspired me and those who showed me what *not* to do. Stories of transformation.

Now, the question is: **What is your story?** And more importantly… **What kind of culture do you want to build?**

When reporters ask successful athletes, CEOs, leaders—anyone worth interviewing—how they achieved success, their answers often sound vague, almost uncomfortable. They give general responses like:

- "I just ran my process."
- "I worked hard to get here."
- "It's all about the team."
- "It's the camaraderie, the mission, the culture we created."

But if you listen carefully, there's a common thread. They're all talking about **culture**.

Success is Never an Accident

Greatness doesn't happen by chance.

It's not just **talent**. Plenty of wickedly talented people fail. It's not just **luck**. Luck without preparation is meaningless. It's not just **ambition**. Plenty of ambitious people never execute.

It's the environment **we create**. It's the rituals, the values, the **behaviors we practice** daily. It's the people we surround ourselves with and the **standards we uphold**.

Every championship team, every high-performing company, every ground-breaking artist has a culture that drives them.

Michael Jordan didn't win six NBA championships because of talent alone—he built a relentless, high-accountability culture around him. Steve Jobs didn't build Apple into a revolutionary company because he had a few good ideas—he embedded innovation into every fiber of the organization.

The Culture You Build is the Legacy You Leave

So, ask yourself:

- What kind of culture do you want to build in your workplace?
- What kind of culture do you foster in your family?
- What kind of energy do you bring into your friendships, your hobbies, your creative projects?

Culture isn't something that exists "out there." It starts within you.

This book has given you the tools, but tools don't build things on their own. **You do**. So, believe in the process, believe in yourself. What will you build? And more importantly... **What will you leave behind?**

FREQUENTLY ASKED QUESTIONS

Before publishing this book, we had 100 beta readers go through it with a fine-tooth comb. We braced ourselves for a flood of questions—some brilliant, some absurd (yes, someone asked if culture could be "too good" and make people soft). After filtering through the most insightful ones, we grouped them here for your reading pleasure.

If you have a question that's personal or unique to your situation, don't hesitate to reach out at **culture@fortesearchpartners.com**. We read every email (and yes, we actually reply).

Q1: How do I keep on track with my personal VIBES?

A1: A famous industrial psychologist once ran an experiment on "deliberate practice" with Harvard MBA grads. He tracked them 10 years post-graduation using income as a success metric.

- **Group A (70%):** Their goal was simply to get a great job and keep an open mind about opportunities.

- **Group B (20%):** They had specific career goals and targeted certain roles.

- **Group C (10%):** They had specific written goals, reviewed them periodically, and adjusted course as needed.

Results 10 years later:

- **Group A:** Earned baseline income (X).
- **Group B:** Earned 2X.
- **Group C:** Earned 10X.

> **LESSON:** *If you don't write your goals down, you are essentially winging it. If you want to 10X your progress, follow the GAFF rule:*

- **Goals:** Be specific. Write them down. No vague aspirations like "I want to be successful." Define success.
- **Action:** A goal without action is just a wish. Break it down into daily, weekly, and monthly steps.
- **Focus:** The top 1% in sports, business, and life share one thing: unbreakable focus. Remove distractions. Stay locked in.
- **Feedback:** The best performers have coaches, mentors, and advisors. Fun fact: I once ran into Serena Williams at a gym—she had three coaches training her simultaneously: one for flexibility, one for strength, and one for cardio endurance. You need at least three, too:

1. A **functional expert** in your field to sharpen your craft.
2. A **confidant** who gives honest, personal feedback.
3. An **accountability coach** who calls you out when you slack.

The best leaders never stop learning. Be a student of the game—always.

Q2: Should we use the culture assessment for candidates pre-hire?

A2: 100% yes. If you don't deliberately hire for culture, you are leaving it to chance. And leaving culture to chance is like planting a garden and hoping weeds don't show up.

Use the **ABC's of Hiring** to get the right people in the door:

- **A - Ability** (*Hard skills*) → Easy to test, easy to teach.

- **B - Behavior** (*Soft skills*) → Harder to test, but essential.
- **C - Culture Fit** (*"Fitting in" skills*) → Medium difficulty to test in interviews, easy with an assessment.

Hiring is not about collecting the best résumés—it's about curating a team that thrives together. If you want a culture of excellence, it starts with who you let in the front door. We have a list of suggested interview questions at the end of this section.

Q3: What if someone in our organization doesn't fit our culture? What should we do?

A3: As Bob (yes, me) said in Part 2, the fastest way to change a company's culture is to change the people. It's not always easy, but it's necessary.

If you tolerate behaviors that don't align with your values, you enable them. Before you know it, you'll have a culture of mediocrity and excuses instead of excellence and ownership.

Here's the hard truth:

Ignoring misaligned employees creates a tolerance for bad behaviors. Tolerance for bad behaviors leads to bad decisions. Bad decisions kill your company's momentum.

Sometimes, misalignment isn't obvious at first. That's why every leader must be culturally aware. If the problem is at the management level, it's even worse—managers tend to hire people who match their own behaviors. A bad-fit leader doesn't just poison culture—they reproduce it.

So, what's the solution?

SPEAK UP. If a leader is hurting the culture, demand change. If no one listens, leave. Staying in a toxic culture that clashes with your values will drain you.

Nothing is more exhausting than working under a bad manager in a broken system. Don't let them turn you into them.

A bad-fit leader doesn't just poison culture—they reproduce it.

Q4: How do I know if I'm choosing the right job at the right company with the right culture?

A4: Do. Your. Homework.

Look, 99% of the time, you can spot whether a company is a cultural dumpster fire during the interview process—but most people ignore the signs because they're too focused on landing the job. It's like dating: the red flags were there, but you convinced yourself they were just "quirks."

Let's talk about science for a second. You know that feeling when you walk out of an interview thinking, "Wow, that just clicked"? That's neuroscience at work. You and the hiring manager were vibing on the same frequency, matching without effort. That's oxytocin—the "trust hormone" —doing its thing.

Now, if you have to force the connection—if the conversation feels awkward, forced, or full of weird pauses—you might be adjusting too hard to their frequency. That's a red flag. Your gut is screaming, "Something's off!" Listen to it.

Red Flags That Scream "RUN!"

Gut Feel Off? If you don't click with the hiring manager, you won't click with the company.

The Culture Question Test: Ask five people the same question: "What's the culture like here?" If you get five completely different answers, there is no culture—just chaos.

Money Bribe: If they keep dangling a big paycheck but can't articulate what makes the job fulfilling, you're being bought—not hired.

No Feedback? If they ghost you after an interview, expect the same treatment when you work there.

Unstructured Process? If the interview feels like it was thrown together five minutes before, so was their business strategy.

Personal Questions? If they ask, "Are you married?" or "Do you plan on having kids soon?"—HUGE NO NO. This is illegal and a sign they don't know (or care about) employment laws.

The best workplaces attract talent, not trap it. If it doesn't feel right, trust your process.

Q5: What's harder to build—personal culture or professional culture?

A5: Easy answer? **Personal culture.**

Why? Because if your personal culture is a mess, your work culture will be, too. You can't build a solid company culture while your own values are crumbling like a Jenga tower.

It's the same reason why airlines tell you to put on your own oxygen mask before helping others. If you're gasping for air, you're no help to anyone.

VIBES is Your Personal Oxygen Mask

Before you fix work, fix yourself:

- **Values:** Define what actually matters to you (not just what looks good on LinkedIn).
- **Interactions:** Do your relationships support you or drain you?
- **Behaviors:** Are your daily habits aligned with your goals?
- **Environment:** Does your space give you energy or stress you out?
- **Success:** Do you measure success based on your standards—or someone else's?

The Identity Crisis Test

If you're one person at home and a completely different person at work, you don't have a work problem—you have an identity problem. And that needs to be solved first.

If you're playing different roles in life, ask yourself: Who am I really?

Once you master your own culture, it's way easier to build it at work.

Bonus PSA: Protect Your Energy

If you're a natural giver, be aware: the world is full of takers. Takers don't just take—they feel entitled to your time, energy, and emotional labor. If you always find yourself overcommitting, set boundaries before you burn out.

Your time, energy, and culture are yours to protect.

So … what kind of culture are YOU building?

Q6: How has COVID changed home life and workplace culture?

A6: I've said this before, but I'll say it again—COVID was the largest social experiment on a planetary scale.

For years, I've been obsessed with adversity—how it makes or breaks people. And after reading hundreds of books, running real-world experiments (yes, I'm that crazy social scientist who loves data), I can confidently say:

Adversity is your best teacher.

It forces us to adapt, reflect, and evolve—or curl up like a turtle and hide in our shell. COVID didn't just shake up our health systems and economies—it exposed our vulnerabilities and forced us to rethink everything.

On the home front, families spent more time together. People experienced loss, fear, and uncertainty, but also connection, resilience, and reinvention. Italians sang on their balconies. Birthdays, weddings, and graduations became drive-by events. The Winter Olympics had cardboard cutouts as an audience (which was both hilarious and terrifying).

On the work front, companies went through the same existential crisis.

Fear-based cultures panicked, froze, and collapsed.

Resilient cultures adapted, thrived, and even grew stronger through the storm.

Everyone else? They're still figuring it out.

Back to neuroscience—humans have three built-in responses to crisis: fight, flight, or freeze. Which one were you?

COVID changed everything. The question is: what did it reveal in you?

Q7: Now that the pandemic is (mostly) over, companies are forcing Return to Office (RTO). What does that mean for culture?

A7: Here's the truth: People don't want to be forced back to the office. They want to be inspired back.

The old-school leaders—the ones who love pacing hallways, popping into cubicles, and "feeling" productivity—want their people back at their desks. The powerful commercial real estate lobbyists (which lost hundreds of billions in rent) are pushing hard to force companies to call their employees to return to the office (RTO).

But here's what the data says: Employees aren't demanding remote work. They're demanding growth.

Polls show that employees prioritize growth and learning over flexibility. That means they will commute IF the workplace adds real value to their lives.

Neuroscience backs this up. Humans are social animals. Like elephants, monkeys, and even ants, we learn better when we're together.

Especially young professionals—they want to experience the culture, build relationships, and be mentored in person.

That doesn't mean we should stroke the egos of leaders who demand but don't inspire. Those leaders? They need to go.

That doesn't mean we should use government intervention to save commercial real estate. The market will correct itself.

What we DO need?

To build cultures where people WANT to be together.

Hybrid work? That's the real answer.

A mix of in-person collaboration and remote flexibility. Less forced mandates and more magnetic culture.

If people love where they work, they'll show up.

Q8: Is there a "best" culture that guarantees success? Like, one culture to rule them all?

A8: Short answer? **No.**

Long answer? If your company's culture doesn't match its business phase, you're setting yourself up for disaster. It's like wearing a tuxedo to a beach party or flip-flops to a black-tie gala—wrong fit, wrong time, wrong results.

Let me tell you a real-life Silicon Valley horror story.

The $100M Misread That Killed a Startup

Two brilliant tech founders—let's call them Steve and Dave—built a promising prototype (Phase 1). They got seed money, tested the product, and had some early traction. Investors threw cash at them because, hey, hot tech sector, right?

Phase 2: They nailed product-market fit (sort of). Early adopters were interested. More funding flowed in. Things were looking good.

Then ... disaster struck.

Phase 2.5 (The "Chasm of Death")

They didn't actually perfect the product. It was clunky, hard to use, and not ready for mass adoption. But instead of fixing it, their board pushed them to scale up immediately.

They went all-in on growth.

- Massive sales hiring spree
- Big-budget rebrand
- Marketing blitz
- Customer success army

They burned through $100M in a year.

But customers weren't sticking because the product wasn't ready. Layoffs followed. Trust evaporated. Culture turned toxic overnight.

What took years to build collapsed in months.

All because they misread their phase and built the wrong culture at the wrong time. And, they were not intentional about what culture they created because they lacked the tools and know-how and relied on a traditional game plan (blindly following the company lifecycle or phases and being out of touch with reality). They were pushed by their board to grow, grow, grow and quickly spiral downward into a zombie startup. So many lives were changed in that rollercoaster year because they allowed their investors/board members' greed to drive them to zombieland. Now they are dying a slow death which is worse than quick death.

Takeaway:

- Be in touch with your company through your customers (actual market) NOT your greed
- Be in touch with your company phase and culture
- Be intentional about your purpose

See the below suggested gameplan to prevent zombieland (or quick death if you're lucky).

BREAKING IT DOWN: MATCHING CULTURE TO BUSINESS PHASE

Phase 1: Seed & Ideation (Culture: Synergy)

The company is basically two engineers in a garage. It's all about collaboration, adaptability, and testing ideas. You need a tight-knit team that thrives on problem-solving.

Phase 2: Early Growth (Culture: Synergy + Spark)

The product is being built, and early customers are giving feedback. This is where innovation is king. The culture needs to be experimental, fast-moving, and hyper-customer-focused.

Phase 2.5: The Chasm (Culture: Synergy + Spark)

The most dangerous phase. If the product is still a pain in the ass to use, early adopters will bail. Companies die here. You either keep listening to customers and refining the product, or you throw money at premature scaling and crash.

Phase 3: Scaling Up (Culture: Spark + Strive)

Now that the product is rock-solid, it's time to invest in growth. Sales, marketing, and customer success go into overdrive. Culture must be aggressive and results-driven, but still innovative.

Phase 4: Maturity & Profitability (Culture: Spark + Structure)

Investors want their return. The company is profitable but must balance efficiency with continued innovation. This is when IPOs, acquisitions, or market expansion happen.

Phase 5: Sustaining Growth (Culture: Structure + Synergy)

If the company stops innovating, it stagnates. This is when companies either acquire smaller, more innovative startups or sell to a bigger player. Culture becomes more corporate, with an emphasis on process and stability.

See the illustration 15 below on the company life cycle.

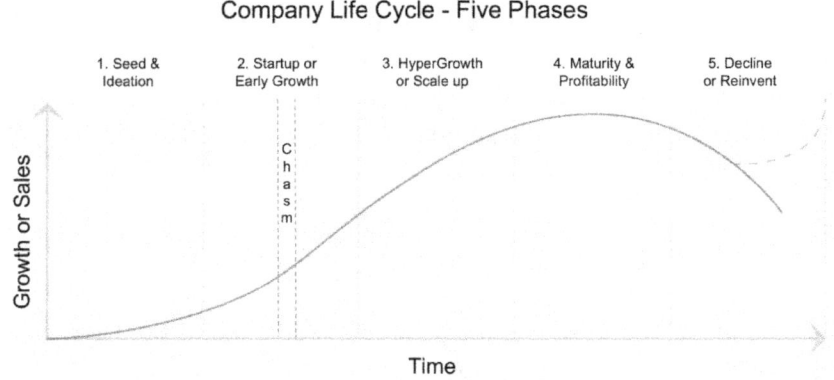

Illustration 15

The Takeaway? Culture Must Evolve.

The mistake most companies make? They try to scale before they're ready.

The best leaders read the phase they're in and adapt their culture accordingly.

Culture isn't one-size-fits-all. It's a living, breathing thing that must grow with the company.

So, before you start building a culture of excellence, ask yourself:

- What phase are we in?
- What kind of culture do we need now?
- Are we moving too fast (or too slow) for where we actually are?

Get that right, and you won't just grow—you'll thrive.

Now, if I were to pick the best culture for long-term success?

High on Synergy & Spark—because companies that take care of their people take care of their customers, and that generates sustainable revenue.

Some Strive—because without a top-notch go-to-market team, the best product in the world won't sell itself.

Appropriate Structure—just enough to create stability without choking innovation.

> **TAKEAWAY:** *Culture is a balancing game that requires leaders to be in touch with it 24/7.*

Take Amazon and Apple. If they had stopped innovating, Private Equity vultures would have gobbled them up, squeezed profits, and left their cultures for dead. Innovation fuels longevity, and it's not just for Product—it should live in Sales, Marketing, Customer Success, Finance, and Operations. Every function should solve hard problems in new ways.

So where do I stand? Quadrants A, B, and C. That's where the magic happens.

Because without Synergy, Spark, and a bit of Strive, even the best companies face a slow, painful death. (And trust me, slow deaths are worse than fast ones.)

The Secret to a Successful Culture – Shhhhhh

There's one **data-backed truth** that companies ignore at their own peril.

Peter Drucker (aka "the father of modern management") had a team tracking what makes companies successful for decades. They built an algorithm that ties variables to share price and found that the #1 indicator of success is…

EMPLOYEE ENGAGEMENT.

Yup. Not market timing. Not product features. Not even competitive advantage. The secret sauce is engaged employees.

A study published in The Wall Street Journal (March 2025) confirmed this with cold, hard data. (See below chart)

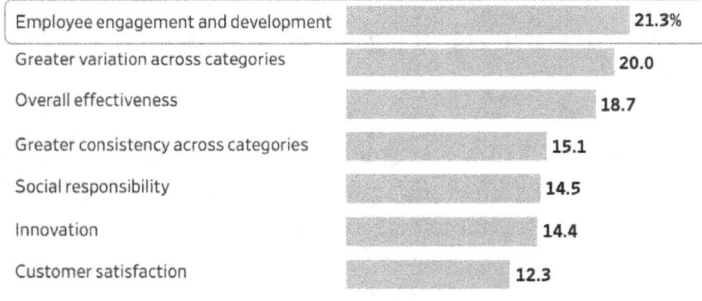

Engagement matters

Average total annual returns, 2013-23, for stock portfolios having certain characteristics, drawn from top-scoring companies in the Drucker rankings

Employee engagement and development	21.3%
Greater variation across categories	20.0
Overall effectiveness	18.7
Greater consistency across categories	15.1
Social responsibility	14.5
Innovation	14.4
Customer satisfaction	12.3

Notes: Each portfolio, which was rebalanced annually, consists of 15 stocks and includes only companies that are part of the S&P 500 index.
Sources: For the portfolio construction and analysis, University of Bern's Jonathan Matzinger, Andreas Hediger, Harley Krohmer and Clemens Ammann, and Claremont Graduate University's David Sprott. For the corporate effectiveness data, Drucker Institute, using data from American Customer Satisfaction Index; American Opportunity Index, a joint project of the Burning Glass Institute, Harvard Business School and the Schultz Family Foundation; Clarivate; CSRHub; Glassdoor; HIP Investor; Indeed; ISS EVA; J.D. Power; Kununu; Lightcast; Payscale; Prof. Dimitris Papanikolaou of Northwestern University and Prof. Amit Seru of Stanford University; Refinitiv Eikon; Supply Chain Resource Cooperative; Sustainalytics; Temkin Group; and wRatings.

Illustration 16

Here's what I've learned from three decades in HR and People Leadership (unlike outside consultants or armchair theorists): 100% of people like to be engaged at work – Nobody wakes up thinking, "I can't wait to be bored and undervalued today!"

Engagement = Growth – If people aren't growing, they're not engaged. When they stagnate, they leave.

Growing = Learning – Companies that prioritize L&D have the highest engagement.

Engagement → Growth → Learning → Retention
→ Happiness → Success (Long-Term).

So, when CEOs cut Learning & Development budgets to save money … guess what?

They just made their employees less engaged, which costs them more money in the long run with higher turnover and less productivity.

Smart leaders get it. They invest in people because they know culture is their biggest competitive advantage.

Culture isn't a buzzword. It's the foundation of long-term success.

The best companies know this. Do you?

Investing in Learning & Development Doesn't Have to Break the Bank

L&D doesn't have to mean expensive executive offsites in Napa, over-the-top leadership retreats, or throwing money at fancy consultants who recycle the same PowerPoint deck for every client. It starts with the basics—small, deliberate actions that compound over time into a culture of continuous learning.

Here's how any company (big or small, startup or legacy) can build a strong L&D culture without burning cash: **Hire Managers Who Are Great Teachers, Mentors & Coaches**

Not all great individual contributors make great managers. Leadership is a separate skillset, and the best leaders are also great teachers, mentors, and coaches.

What's the difference?

- **Teachers** → Share knowledge and develop technical skills.
- **Mentors** → Provide guidance, wisdom, and career advice.
- **Coaches** → Push people to perform, grow, and hold them accountable.

Great managers prioritize learning, not just output. If your managers aren't teaching, mentoring, or coaching their teams, they're just glorified taskmasters.

Build a Mentoring Program (Cheap, Effective, Game-Changing)

Mentorship doesn't require a huge budget—just intentionality. Pair junior employees with experienced mentors. Set clear goals. Encourage reverse mentoring so knowledge flows both ways.

Why?

- **Mentees accelerate their growth.**
- **Mentors strengthen their leadership skills.**
- **Employees stay longer because they feel invested in.**

> **PRO TIP:** *The best mentor-mentee relationships aren't forced. Give people options and let organic connections form.*

> **PRO TIP:** *Hire locally for junior-level people, they learn much better in person than Zooming via video.*

Make "Teaching the Teacher" a Standard for Career Growth

Too many companies treat career progression as a checklist of tasks. Instead, they should ask:

"Can this person teach, mentor, or coach someone else?"

The best way to grow into leadership is to help others grow. Individual contributors should be required to mentor and teach junior employees before moving up.

HR doesn't need to reinvent the wheel—just run a Teach the Teacher program.

- Train high-potential employees on how to teach and mentor.
- Recognize and reward those who do it well.
- Make it a promotion requirement.

Teaching solidifies knowledge, builds confidence, and strengthens culture.

Leaders, Managers & ICs Should Each Mentor At Least 2 People.

The best cultures don't leave mentorship to chance—they make it part of their DNA.

- Every executive should mentor at least 2 people.
- Every manager should mentor at least 2 people.
- Every high-performing IC should mentor at least 2 people.

This builds what Ava's company calls a "Learning & Growing Culture." When mentorship becomes a cultural expectation, knowledge-sharing becomes second nature, and the entire company levels up.

FINAL THOUGHT: THE COMPOUNDING EFFECT OF LEARNING CULTURE

Companies often overcomplicate L&D. They pour millions into training programs but ignore the everyday interactions that actually shape learning.

The secret?

- Hire managers who love to teach.
- Make mentorship an expectation, not a side project.
- Turn knowledge-sharing into a habit, not a one-off initiative.

The best companies aren't just learning organizations—they're teaching organizations.

Want to build a great culture? Start by hiring learners and growing great people.

Q9: *What kind of leadership actually creates a great culture?*

A9: Ever wonder why Phil Jackson and Steve Kerr—two of the most successful basketball coaches of all time—were able to build dynasties while other equally talented coaches flamed out?

It's simple. They weren't just coaches. They were leaders who played the game themselves.

Jackson and Kerr weren't obsessed with individual stats or ego-driven power moves. They focused on teaching, inspiring, and creating a winning culture. They understood that championships are won by teams, not just star players.

In business? The best leaders are "player-coaches."

They don't just bark orders from the sidelines. They know the mechanics of the game, have walked the path, and lead by example. They empower their team, trust their people, and understand that winning is a team sport.

After working with, hiring, and (yes) firing many leaders, one leadership style consistently outperforms the rest: inspirational leadership.

These leaders:

- **Coach, don't control:** They develop talent instead of micromanaging.
- **Put the team first:** They don't chase personal glory; they build organizations that last.
- **Show up in tough times:** They don't play the blame game or hide when things get hard.

THE LEADERSHIP STYLES THAT BUILD A STRONG CULTURE (PURPOSE-BASED)

The Inspirational Leader

- **Coaches, not controls:** They develop talent instead of micromanaging.
- **Puts the team first:** They don't chase personal glory; they build organizations that last.
- **Shows up in tough times:** They don't play the blame game or disappear when things get hard.
- **Communicates with clarity and purpose:** They make sure everyone understands the "why," not just the "what."

The Servant Leader

- **Empowers instead of commands:** They remove obstacles so their team can thrive.
- **Listens before leading:** They seek input, understand concerns, and act with humility.

- **Leads with empathy:** They know that great performance comes from people who feel valued.
- **Prioritizes long-term success over short-term wins:** They don't sacrifice culture for quick results.

The Growth-Oriented Leader

- **Encourages continuous learning:** They challenge their team to grow without fear of failure.
- **Fosters psychological safety:** People take risks because mistakes aren't punished—they're learned from.
- **Invests in people:** They mentor, coach, and create future leaders.
- **Adapts and evolves:** They aren't stuck in "this is how we've always done it" mode.

The Visionary Leader

- Inspires through a shared mission – They get people excited about the bigger picture.
- Sees possibilities, not just problems – They push boundaries and embrace innovation.
- **Balances vision with execution:** Dreaming big is great, but they also get shit done.
- **Brings energy and optimism:** Their passion is contagious, and they rally people behind a cause.

The Adaptive Leader *(The One Who Thrives in Chaos)*

- **Reads the room:** They assess people, situations, and market changes in real time.
- **Leads with agility:** They pivot when necessary, without losing sight of the bigger picture.

- **Balances stability with flexibility :** They maintain core values but adjust strategies as needed.
- **Knows that no one leadership style fits all:** They adapt their approach based on the needs of their team and business.

Great leaders don't force people into a rigid mold. They understand the moment, the mission, and the team, and they adapt to bring out the best in everyone.

Because at the end of the day?

Leadership isn't about being the loudest voice in the room. It's about creating a culture where people can do their best work.

The Common Thread? Trust.

All great leaders build trust.

Trust fuels culture.

Culture drives performance.

When leaders focus on inspiration over intimidation, empowerment over micromanagement, and vision over ego—that's when real magic happens.

Now, let's talk about what doesn't work.

THE LEADERSHIP STYLES THAT KILL CULTURE (FEAR-BASED)

The Ego-Driven Tyrant

These leaders make great first impressions—especially on boards and investors—but behind closed doors? They treat people like disposable assets. They read the latest fad leadership books, preach "vision" and "culture," but when things go south? They fire people instead of fixing the root problem. Their motto: *Protect my reputation at all costs.*

The Command-and-Control General

Some industries (think military, finance, manufacturing) require strict discipline, but in fast-moving, innovative fields like tech? This style is a disaster. When a leader is obsessed with control, approvals, and hierarchy, creativity dies, decision-making slows to a crawl, and morale tanks. The worst leaders? They care more about pleasing the board than leading their teams. They make short-term, fear-driven decisions that protect their own status instead of investing in people.

The Passive-Aggressive Avoider

This is the leader who smiles to your face but never gives direct feedback. They hate conflict, so they let toxic behaviors slide—until one day, they snap and make a rash, emotional decision. They create an environment where nothing gets addressed head-on, accountability is weak, and passive-aggressiveness spreads like wildfire. Their motto: *If I ignore it long enough, maybe it'll go away.* Spoiler: It never does.

The Data-Obsessed Robot

Numbers don't lie, but people aren't numbers. This leader only cares about spreadsheets, KPIs, and analytics. They love metrics so much they forget that culture isn't quantifiable. If a decision looks good on paper but destroys morale, they still go through with it. These leaders often cut essential people to save a percentage point on the balance sheet—then wonder why the company loses its magic.

The Superhero Micromanager

This leader thinks they're saving the company, but they're actually suffocating it. They swoop in, take over projects, rewrite emails, and redo presentations because "it's just easier if I do it myself." They create learned helplessness—their team stops making decisions because they know the boss will override them anyway. Over time, the best employees leave for autonomy, and the ones who stay become passive order-takers.

The Fixed Mindset Fossil

These leaders believe success is a one-time achievement, not a continuous process. They resist change, dismiss new ideas, and stick to what worked in the past—even when it clearly no longer does. They're the ones who say, *"We've always done it this way."* Their organizations stagnate because they refuse to adapt, and their teams feel stuck in a time warp. Meanwhile, their more agile competitors pass them by. Their motto: *If it ain't broke, don't fix it.* Reality check: *It's already breaking.*

The Common Thread? Insecurity.

All these leadership styles come from a place of fear.

- Fear of losing control.
- Fear of looking bad.
- Fear of failing.

I've worked for CEOs who embodied one (or sometimes a toxic cocktail of all) of these leadership styles. Finding a truly inspirational leader was like spotting a unicorn—rare and almost mythical. The leaders to avoid? The ones who hate losing more than they love winning. They operate from fear, not inspiration. Fear-based leaders make reactive, short-sighted decisions, stifle creativity, and micromanage to maintain control. Inspire-based leaders cultivate trust, push boundaries, and rally people around a vision that makes them want to win together. The difference? One leads by fear. The other leads by purpose.

THE BEST LEADERS?

- They empower instead of control.
- They trust instead of micromanage.
- They focus on long-term impact, not short-term optics.

Great culture starts with great leadership. And great leadership starts with self-awareness.

But Here's the Good News:

The **next generation of leaders**—Millennials (like Ava in the story) and Gen Z—are changing the game.

Within a few years, they will make up two-thirds of the workforce. And they care about purpose, culture, and leadership that actually values people.

The future belongs to leaders who inspire.

The question is: What kind of leader do you want to be?

CLOSING THOUGHTS: CULTURE IS EVERYTHING

This book represents my experiences, my failures, my breakthroughs, and the lessons I've gathered along the way. The stories I've shared? They're my opinions, my perspective—shaped by three decades of building cultures, learning from great leaders, and witnessing firsthand what works (and what absolutely doesn't).

You may agree with some ideas. You may challenge others. That's a good thing. Culture isn't a rigid formula—it's alive, evolving, and deeply personal. But one truth stands firm:

Culture drives success.

Not luck. Not talent alone. Not just hard work.

Culture is the invisible force that determines whether a team thrives or crumbles, whether a company innovates or stagnates, whether a leader builds a legacy or leaves destruction in their wake.

Culture isn't just some corporate buzzword—it's an organic, biological, and deeply human thing. It exists whether you cultivate it or not. The question is: Are you shaping your culture, or is it shaping you?

There is a process to building inspirational, strong, and moral cultures. (And yes—stay tuned for my next book, where I'll unwrap "The Process" in full detail.)

But for now, here's my final ask of you:

- **Be intentional:** Culture doesn't happen by accident—it happens by design.
- **Be bold:** Change doesn't come from playing it safe.
- **Be the leader you wish you had:** Whether in your workplace, your home, or your community.

My intention with this book is simple: To share my knowledge and inspire generations to be their best selves—at home and at work. Because at the end of the day, that's what culture is about: people, values, and the legacy we choose to leave behind.

So go out there. Build something meaningful. Shape the culture you want to see. And most importantly—**never stop growing.**

SAMPLE CULTURE INTERVIEW QUESTIONS

By now, you've read the book, done the exercises, and started designing an intentional personal and professional culture.

Now, let's talk about hiring the right people to sustain that culture.

Why Culture-Driven Hiring Matters

I firmly believe that a growth mindset fuels a growth culture. And as you've learned:

$$Engagement \rightarrow Growth \rightarrow Learning \rightarrow Retention \\ \rightarrow Happiness \rightarrow Success\ (Long\text{-}Term)$$

Hiring isn't just about filling roles—it's about finding the right people who align with your mission, values, and long-term vision.

I started my career in HR/People as a recruiter, and I've hired (and, yes, fired) many recruiters in my time. Even the best make hiring mistakes. Even monkeys fall from trees.

If a hire fits the culture, it's magic. If they don't? It's painful for them, their manager, and the entire team.

That's why hiring for culture is just as critical as hiring for skill.

The 3 Levels of Hiring - Back to the ABC's

- **A - Abilities or Technical Skills?** Easy to assess. Either they have them or they don't.
- **B- Behaviors or Soft Skills?** Harder. You need the right questions and assessments to evaluate them properly.
- **C- Culture Fit?** The hardest. Without a structured process (like the 4-S Assessment), you're just guessing.

The Cost of a Bad Hire:

- Individual contributors → 2x their salary
- People Managers → 5x their salary
- VPs & Executives → 10x their salary

Moral of the story: Hire with intention. A bad hire is a culture killer.

Culture Interview Questions

To help you **hire for values, behaviors, and culture,** here are some **tested, real-life questions** I've used successfully in my career.

Growth & Development

"In our company, we prioritize continuous growth and development. What are you currently doing for your own self-development? What do you expect from us to help you grow?"

Personal Values & Alignment

"Pick five values that are important to you and explain why. Please write them down and take your time."

Learning from Failure

"Tell me about a time you failed at something. How did you handle it, and what did you learn?"

Ownership & Accountability

"Give me an example of a time you took extreme ownership of a project, even when it wasn't technically your responsibility."

Work & Team Culture

"What type of culture brings out your best performance? What type of culture frustrates you?"

More Culture Interview Questions by Quadrant

Hiring for culture fit is **not a one-size-fits-all approach**. Different roles naturally lean toward different cultural quadrants in the 4-S Model:

- **Synergy** (Collaboration & People-Centric)
- **Spark** (Innovation & Creativity)
- **Strive** (Performance & Competition)
- **Structure** (Process & Stability)

Below are five additional culture interview questions designed to help you assess the cultural alignment of your candidates based on the role they're applying for.

Synergy Culture Questions (Best for Customer Success, HR, Admin roles)

People in Synergy-driven cultures thrive in collaborative, people-focused environments. They prioritize teamwork, relationships, and creating a sense of belonging.

"Describe a time you went out of your way to help a teammate or customer. What was the impact?"

"Tell me about a time when you had to collaborate with a difficult personality. How did you handle it?"

"How do you personally contribute to fostering a positive and inclusive work environment?"

"What does 'psychological safety' mean to you, and how do you create it in a team?"

"If two teammates had a conflict, how would you mediate and resolve it?"

Spark Culture Questions (Best for Engineers, Marketing, Product roles)

People in Spark-driven cultures thrive on creativity, problem-solving, and pushing boundaries. They challenge norms and think outside the box.

"Give an example of a time you challenged the status quo. What happened?"

"What's a creative idea you pitched that got rejected? How did you respond?"

"How do you balance innovation with practicality when building solutions?"

"If you were given unlimited time and budget, what's a project or product you'd love to create?"

"Tell me about a time when you failed at something new. What did you learn, and how did you iterate?"

Strive Culture Questions (Best for Sales, Marketing, Customer Success, C-Levels)

People in Strive-driven cultures are motivated by competition, performance, and achieving results. They have grit, resilience, and a winning mindset.

"Describe a time when you had to push past rejection or failure to achieve success."

"What motivates you more—winning as an individual or winning as a team? Why?"

"Give an example of a time you exceeded your goals. What drove you to go beyond expectations?"

"How do you handle high-pressure situations, and what strategies do you use to stay focused?"

"Tell me about a time when you had to outwork or outsmart a competitor. How did you do it?"

Structure Culture Questions (Best for CEO, CFO, COO, CSO, Finance, Legal, Ops roles)

People in Structure-driven cultures value stability, efficiency, and clear processes. They keep things organized, compliant, and scalable.

"Describe a time when you implemented a process that improved efficiency or reduced risk."

"What's your approach to balancing structure with flexibility in a fast-changing environment?"

"How do you ensure compliance without slowing down innovation or progress?"

"Tell me about a time when you had to enforce a rule or policy that was unpopular. How did you handle it?"

"If you were given an unstructured department with no processes in place, what would be your first steps?"

A strong culture isn't about hiring one type of person—it's about hiring the right mix of Synergy, Spark, Strive, and Structure to keep the organization balanced and thriving.

Use these quadrant-based culture interview questions to ensure your team has the right cultural DNA.

UNCONVENTIONAL INTERVIEW QUESTIONS BY CULTURE QUADRANT

Most interview questions are predictable and rehearsed. The best way to truly understand how a candidate thinks, reacts, and fits into your culture? Ask them situational questions they didn't expect. Below are five unconventional, out-of-the-box interview questions tailored for each 4-S culture quadrant.

Synergy (Collaboration & People-Centric)

(Best for Customer Success, HR, Admin roles—focus on emotional intelligence, teamwork, and empathy.)

"If you had to build a community from scratch on a deserted island, what's the first rule you'd put in place?" (Reveals how they prioritize structure, fairness, and collaboration.)

"Tell me about a time you made someone's day at work. What happened?" (Shows their natural inclination for kindness, culture-building, and teamwork.)

"Imagine I'm your teammate, and I just made a huge mistake that affects our whole team. How do you handle it?" (Tests their conflict resolution skills and approach to accountability.)

"If we gave you a budget to improve company culture, but you couldn't spend it on perks like food or events, how would you use it?" (Measures their creative thinking on fostering engagement beyond surface-level incentives.)

"You wake up tomorrow and discover you can read minds. How would you use this new power at work?" (A fun way to gauge their ethics, leadership mindset, and interpersonal approach.)

Spark (Innovation & Creativity)

(Best for Engineers, Marketing, Product roles—focus on out-of-the-box thinking, problem-solving, and adaptability.)

"If you had to design a completely useless app that millions of people would still download, what would it do?" (Tests creativity and understanding of human behavior.)

"You're given a blank check to reinvent one of our products or processes. What's the first thing you'd change?" (Shows innovation instincts and risk-taking appetite.)

"If aliens landed tomorrow and wanted to invest in our company, how would you pitch our product to them?" (Measures storytelling, improvisation, and ability to simplify complex ideas.)

"**If you could shadow any historical innovator (dead or alive) for a week, who would it be and why?**" (Reveals who inspires them and how they think about progress.)

"**Imagine your job disappeared tomorrow. How would you pivot your skills into a brand-new career?**" (Tests adaptability and self-awareness in a rapidly changing world.)

Strive (Performance & Competition)

(Best for Sales, Marketing, Customer Success, C-Levels—focus on ambition, resilience, and competitive drive.)

"**If you had to sell me a broken pen in 30 seconds, how would you do it?**" (Classic sales test—reveals their persuasion skills and ability to think on their feet.)

"**Describe the last time you genuinely hated losing. What did you do afterward?**" (Shows their resilience and how they handle setbacks.)

"**You're in a race, and you overtake the person in second place. What position are you in now?**" (Tests attention to detail and ability to think quickly under pressure.)

"**If you had a billboard in Times Square with one sentence to describe your professional brand, what would it say?**" (Reveals self-awareness and how they perceive their own value.)

"**You have one minute to convince me you deserve a 50% higher salary than what we're offering. Go.**" (Assesses confidence, negotiation skills, and self-worth.)

Structure (Process & Stability)

(Best for CEO, CFO, COO, CSO, Finance, Legal, Ops—focus on efficiency, risk management, and systems thinking.)

"You walk into a room with three doors. One leads to a lava pit, one to a lion that hasn't eaten in three years, and one to a booby-trapped hallway. Which one do you choose and why?" (Tests logical thinking and problem-solving under constraints.)

"If you had to cut our operating costs by 20% without laying off a single person, how would you do it?" (Measures strategic decision-making and financial acumen.)

"A colleague consistently misses deadlines, slowing down your team's work. How do you address it?" (Reveals leadership style and how they handle accountability.)

"Describe a process you created or improved that saved significant time or money." (Shows real-world impact and operational efficiency.)

"If you could only track three KPIs to measure company success, which would you choose and why?" (Tests their ability to prioritize data-driven decision-making.)

CANDIDATE CULTURE FIT GUIDE

10 Smart Questions Candidates Should Ask to Evaluate Company Culture

1. "How would you describe the company culture in five words?" (Pay attention to consistency across interviewers.)

2. "Can you share a recent example of a cultural value in action?" (Stories beat slogans. If they can't name one, culture may be performative.)

3. "What behavior gets rewarded here—and what gets penalized?" (This cuts to the real values beneath the poster values.)

4. "What do team rituals or traditions look like?" (Do they sound human and joyful or corporate and forced?)

5. "What kind of people tend to succeed here—and who tends to struggle?" (This gives insight into unwritten rules.)

6. **"How does the company support learning and development?"** (A culture of growth invests in its people.)

7. **"When the company faces challenges, how does leadership respond?"** (You'll learn about transparency, trust, and values under pressure.)

8. **"What's one thing you'd change about the company culture if you could?"** (This reveals honesty—and possible red flags.)

9. **"How do cross-functional teams collaborate here?"** (Watch for signs of silos, politics, or blame games.)

10. **"How has the culture evolved over the last couple of years?"** (Culture should evolve as the company grows.)

Culture Fit Flags: Green, Yellow, and Red

Green Flag: Strong Fit, Clear Culture

- Interviewers give consistent answers to culture questions.
- You hear real stories tied to values.
- Culture is aligned with your values and working style.
- You leave energized and see yourself thriving there.

Yellow Flag: Mixed Signals, Unclear Alignment

- Interviewers give different answers about the culture.
- Some answers feel generic or rehearsed.
- You feel uncertain about how decisions are made or how success is defined.
- You're not sure how your values align with theirs.

Red Flag: Culture is Unclear or Contradictory

- Interviewers can't clearly articulate the company culture.

- Responses are buzzword-heavy but substance-light.
- There's no sign of values in action—just posters and PowerPoints.
- You feel like you'd have to shapeshift to fit in.

> REMEMBER: *You're not just being interviewed—you're interviewing them too. The best hiring decisions are mutual decisions. Your future self will thank you for doing the cultural due diligence now.*

More Culture Interview Questions

For additional questions and a full culture hiring guide, visit our website and download it for free at **www.fortesearchpartners.com**

Bottom Line: Culture is intentional. So is hiring.

The wrong person can break a team. The right person can elevate an entire company.

Hire wisely.

I believe so much in the topic that I built an assessment (free to the reader), wrote books, taught it (at Stanford Continuing Studies), and placed—and continue to place—inspirational leaders in culture-conscience organizations.

Stay tuned for more information about the next set of books, one which is focused on how to demystify and unwrap what top performers refer to as "The Process." The other is focused on how to hire for culture.

BONUS SECTION: THE RECIPE FOR A CULTURE OF EXCELLENCE

For the Culture Chefs Who Want to Cook with Confidence

So many of our early readers, clients, and culture nerds wrote in asking the same thing:

"This book is amazing—but can you just give me a recipe I can follow step-by-step?"

We heard you.

This bonus section is for all the CEOs, HR leaders, founders, and people managers who are ready to roll up their sleeves and cook up something truly great—but need a bit of help getting started.

Think of this as your **Culture Cookbook**. A universal recipe that outlines the key ingredients, order of operations, and techniques to build an inspirational, sustainable, high-performing culture.

But here's the catch: **Culture is organic.** It's alive. It breathes. It changes with every new person, every strategy shift, every market jolt. So, while this recipe gives you structure, you still have to taste-test and adjust as you go.

Just like every great dish, it needs seasoning, intuition, and love.

So, whether you're launching a new startup, scaling a rocket ship, or fixing a soggy soufflé of a company culture—this section is your mise en place.

Let's get cooking.

Culture: The Secret Sauce of Every Great Company

If strategy is the brain, operations are the hands, and mission is the heart—then culture is the soul. It's the secret sauce that flavors everything: how people treat each other, how customers are supported, how decisions get made when nobody's watching. Culture is the glue. The yeast in the bread. The seasoning that brings bland spaghetti (aka a company with smart people and no soul) to life.

Let's cook this thing right.

STEP-BY-STEP RECIPE FOR BUILDING A SUSTAINABLE CULTURE OF EXCELLENCE

Step 1: Run the Culture Diagnostic (The Taste Test)

Tool: 4-S Culture Assessment

Before you cook a gourmet meal, you need to taste your ingredients. Where is your culture today? Where do you want it to be? The 4-S assessment helps you figure that out.

- NOW = **Current state** (aka, what's in the fridge)
- PREFERRED = **Ideal state** (what you'd *like* to serve guests)

Action Items:

- Have all leaders and extended leadership team take the 4-S
- Analyze results by team, function, and seniority level
- Identify culture gaps, misalignments, and subcultures
- Determine if your company is stuck in a quadrant (e.g. too much Structure, not enough Spark)

Step 2: Write Your Culture Statement (Your House Recipe)

Create a bold, aspirational, values-based statement that describes your **future culture.** This is your **"North Star."** Make it short, punchy, and memorable.

> **EXAMPLE:** *"We are a culture of builders, learners, and givers. We take care of each other, challenge the status quo, and deliver results with heart."*

Action Items:

- Co-create it with the leadership team

- Gut-check with employees—do they feel inspired or just confused?
- Post it everywhere (walls, handbooks, onboarding, Slack bios)

Step 3: Align Leadership (The Head Chefs)

Culture doesn't belong to HR. It belongs to the CEO. And it must be **co-owned by every single leader.**

Action Items:

- Identify culture champions within leadership
- Set clear expectations (e.g. every leader mentors two people, runs value-based team rituals, etc.)
- Build cultural ownership into OKRs or performance plans
- Require that values are demonstrated, not just memorized

> **REMINDER:** *If your leaders are misaligned, the dish gets burned. Culture can't taste like garlic in Sales and vanilla in Engineering.*

Step 4: Conduct a People Strategy Audit (The Pantry Inventory)

Your **People team** is the sous-chef. They don't cook the meal, but they prep the ingredients and make sure you have the right tools.

Action Items:

- Audit current people programs (hiring, onboarding, performance, development, feedback loops)
- Align all HR touchpoints to reflect your culture quadrant priorities (see Synergy, Spark, Strive, Structure)
- Create a Programmatic People Strategy (PPS) to track initiatives tied to business goals

> **EXAMPLE:** *If you want more Spark, introduce peer innovation days, learning stipends, and experimentation labs. If you want more Synergy, invest in mentorship and manager coaching.*

Step 5: Hire for Culture Add, Not Culture Fit (Your New Ingredients)

Stop hiring people just because they "feel like us." That leads to mono-culture soup. Instead, hire for **culture**—add people who bring new flavor while sharing your values.

Action Items:

- **Use ABC hiring process:** Ability, Behavior, Culture
- Add values-based interview questions
- Involve team members in the process—culture is communal
- Use the pre-hire culture assessment

Step 6: Design Rituals & Rhythms (The Secret Spices)

Culture is built in **moments**. Rituals turn values into habits. You want a few signature moves that **signal who you are**.

Ideas:

- Weekly "Failure Fridays" or "What I Learned" sharing sessions
- Monthly value dinners hosted by execs
- **Walk-and-talk 1:1s** instead of stale Zooms
- Surprise gratitude shoutouts from peers

Don't over-orchestrate. Keep it organic. Let teams create their own flavors.

Step 7: Measure Culture Quarterly (Taste as You Go)

This isn't a "set it and forget it" slow cooker. Culture changes with every new hire, exit, reorg, or leadership shift.

Action Items:

- Retake the 4-S assessment every 3–6 months
- Do mini pulse surveys (3 questions, 3 minutes)
- Track VIBES scores at the individual or team level
- Run skip-level feedback sessions
- Add cultural metrics to your board decks

What gets measured gets managed. What gets ignored gets weird.

Step 8: Build Feedback Loops (The Taste Testers)

Make feedback a part of your operating system. You want **real-time cultural intelligence**, not a surprise stomachache at year-end reviews.

Action Items:

- Train managers to give and receive feedback using VIBES
- Open anonymous channels (but don't rely on them)
- Coach employees to speak up directly—with kindness and clarity

Step 9: Celebrate the Right People (Your House Specials)

People will model what you reward. So, if you celebrate heroes who embody your values, others will follow.

Action Items:

- Create a "Values in Action" award
- Shout out role models in All Hands meetings
- Tie recognition and promotion to cultural contribution

> **WARNING:** *If you only reward performance and ignore behavior, you'll end up with toxic all-stars and eroded trust.*

Step 10: Embed Culture into Strategy (The Whole Damn Kitchen)

Culture isn't frosting. It's the batter. It should show up in every company decision—from pricing to customer service to how meetings run.

Action Items:

- Use culture as a filter for all strategic choices
- Train execs to "pressure-test" strategies against values
- Make culture reviews part of business reviews

CULTURE COOK'S FINAL THOUGHT:

Culture isn't what you say. It's what you consistently do. It's the pattern. The VIBE. The feeling when someone joins your Video Conference room or walks through your office.

Follow this recipe and you'll create more than a company. You'll build a movement. A place people want to belong to. A workplace that feels like home for your best self.

So put on your apron, grab your ingredients, and fire up the stove. Your culture won't cook itself.

ACKNOWLEDGMENTS

I'd like to express gratitude to the many individuals who have played a role in shaping who I am.

Thank you to my mother for instilling resilience and strength. To my sister, for emphasizing the importance of family. My brother has shown me how to strive for personal growth and demonstrate affection for family members, including our canine ones. I appreciate the support of my uncles, aunt, cousins, and nieces. I love you all.

My work colleagues (and bosses) have been instrumental in encouraging my development as a leader, aiming to lead with head, heart, and spirit. To Michelle, for partnering on the next professional journey, it's a lot less scary together. To my high school buddy, Dave who continues to cheer me on and teach me how to be bold and take chances with the next phase of life and career.

My wife deserves special mention. She embodies love and beauty and is my life partner and inspiration. I am grateful for our journey together. You've been the greatest friend, teacher, mother and my everything in life. My two daughters have challenged me to be a better father and are a source of love and fulfillment.

I believe that relationships are the real currency in life. That is what culture is all about.

Babak "Bob" Dehnad is the kind of guy who believes culture isn't just a buzzword—it's the secret sauce. A seasoned executive in Silicon Valley's People/HR trenches, Babak has spent decades obsessing over what makes companies thrive (hint: it's not just snacks and swag). As a self-proclaimed social scientist, he's run real-life experiments—disguised as HR programs—to prove that "culture drives success" (also the name of his YouTube channel, where he preaches the gospel of vibes with data). He's led talent strategy through IPOs, acquisitions, and every startup surprise in between. These days, he's the Chief Partner of Forte Search Partners, a culture-based retained executive search firm helping leaders hire the right leaders. He also moonlights as a Stanford Continuing Studies instructor, teaching others how to build cultures that actually work.

Oh—and in case you're wondering, yes: he's the real "Bob" in this book.

www.ingramcontent.com/pod-product-compliance
Lightning Source LLC
Chambersburg PA
CBHW062319120626
46546CB00013B/1852